CONFIDENCE
MASTERY
FOR
COUPLES

Roadmap to a More
Intimate Relationship

CONFIDENCE
MASTERY
FOR
COUPLES

Roadmap to a More
Intimate Relationship

MELINDA VAN FLEET

Good Karma Confidence™ Series - I

Thriving Communication Press™
Tavernier, Florida

Special thank you to my editor - Valerie Costa of Costa Creative Services
Contact at valerie@costacreativeservices.com

Library of Congress Number - 2021902303

ISBN 978-1-7365917-0-3 Paperback
ISBN 978-1-7365917-1-0 eBook
ISBN 978-1-7365917-2-7 Audible

Printed in the United States of America.

Cover Design by 100Covers.com
Interior Design by FormattedBooks.com

Dedication

To Ryan:

Well......what can I say? When I started on this venture to begin writing a series on confidence using our stories, you didn't look at me and say no. In our world, that's a go. I am thankful for your unwavering support and that I know the drill.

The journey we have been on and continue to be on is above and beyond what we both expected in our lives. And a lot of it is shared in this book. I am grateful you are open to that and hope the world is as well.

I am also grateful for your love, honesty, and openness to work on yourself as equally as helping me to be a better person. I knew the moment we met that we were a team and nothing could break us. We have each other's back through all the bad times and the good times. You make me laugh, think of things through a different lens, and allow me to be myself. You have even more to offer this world and I hope you know your love is appreciated!

I love you-

Melinda

Contents

Introduction

"If you don't stop acting like your mother, I am leaving you."

My heart stopped. It likely flatlined for a few seconds. I stood in our tiny kitchen in Minneapolis, MN, as time stood still, and I was speechless. I stared at Ryan as he stood there with determination and strength in conveying his message. Believe me when I say that I heard it loud and clear.

Imagine your husband says this to you. We were married for a little over a year and were about to leave on vacation to Mexico. A break we were excited to take. A small discussion about something stupid turned into a mind-blowing, life-changing declaration.

In the same flash of shock, I also saw awareness. I felt as if the skies opened up to provide clarity as to why I was often struggling with people, work, and relationships. In that instant, it became clear. As if a big beam of lightning struck me.

My entire career was laden with underlying struggles of work relationships. In my 20s, I was extremely competitive. In every review I was told, "Melinda, just worry about yourself. You are very talented, but you need to learn to work with other people." I was fired from a large corporation and struggled within that corporation so much that I lost 20 pounds from the stress. Getting fired was a relief, as often it is- truth! However, I then went to work for another corporation and struggled with my team there, as well.

I also had a tough time dating. Judgment, unrealistic expectations, and a nasty tone were some of the reasons I struggled, but I never saw it. I had no idea I behaved in such a fashion. No one had ever stood up to me and called me out on my shit. But my husband did. I was shocked, but in a way - proud.

This book isn't about my mother. However, there are stories that relate back to my mother as my growth is part of recognizing where a lot of the behavior has come from, and it's my story. It would be inauthentic to not share those stories, and I know that they can help someone else.

This book is also about challenges that we all have which can be overcome with recognizing them and building habits that create change. Recognizing and owning your issues is a huge step. And, owning your issues is a lot less stressful than being a victim, martyr, or covering them up. It's also more authentic and part of being a good person.

My husband, Ryan, is a beautiful soul. He is kind, funny, intelligent, and open to ideas and change. I followed my intuition when we first met. I knew the second I saw him that we were supposed to be together. I knew he would never hurt me, and we had the same passion and overall goals.

I remember my dad saying for our wedding toast, "You guys will be fine because you are both hard workers." Not necessarily a toast one gives their daughter; however, it has proven to be true.

There were times in which if I didn't love him so much, I would have thrown in the towel because Ryan's behavior was so challenging. But, I was not aware of how much he was living in the past and how that was affecting his confidence, which affected our relationship. His internal pain of reliving the past was worse than I recognized.

We all have strengths and weaknesses. And I am sure you have heard, "It takes two to tango."

Personally, and as a coach, I have learned that often one person blames the other. But it's not always an accurate picture. More often, our lives intertwine and our souls have even been together before at one point or another. Therefore, we are brought together again to help each other, strengthen each other, and uplift each other. I am not a PhD, therapist, or psychologist, but an average person going through many challenges that we all face.

We are also here to celebrate each other's wins, be supportive through the struggle, and bring light to darkness and misunderstanding. Each day presents a new challenge, but also a new opportunity to grow. We all have daily challenges that may be outside of our control. This can easily play with our mindset and confidence. What goes on in our heads can be the most confusing and difficult nut to crack because it takes communication. But, even before that, it takes recognizing.

This book is from a place of compassion, confidence, and communication, which I believe are the three pillars to building a successful relationship. My positive mindset is a combination of being wired this way and years of work in learning how to quickly change my thought patterns. I intend to share those tips and tools with you in this book.

You may notice here and there that I repeat action steps and topics. It has been proven, and I have learned from experience, that repetition over time is what creates change. The topics may intertwine; hence, again, the repetition. We all have limiting beliefs from when we were children. But, those limiting beliefs can be changed. Intuitively, if you didn't believe that thought process you would not be reading this book. Hence, I believe you have the power to change, as well.

This book is a tool for you and your partner to achieve success in every way possible. I start most chapters with self-reflecting questions. We rarely stop to take a moment to think about where we are. The questions are meant for each of you to think about and discuss. You may be the person reading this book, but then take what you need as a tool for open communication. It is likely you will not sit and read this book together. That doesn't happen in our household. But, I do find ways to sneak the discussion in. And heck, we all often need productive things to talk about besides, "Did you take the dogs out yet?" So here is your opportunity for better communication and discussion.

Think of this book like your favorite cookbook. You have it on your bookshelf and remember various aspects and stories that you pull out and relate to over time. You may read this book now and perhaps not all of the chapters or stories will resonate with you. But when something happens in your life or relationship, you can grab it and can flip to the chapter that relates. Many of the books I own and have read have become tools that have helped me grow. This book can do the same for you.

At the end of the book, I share more tips and tools to use to help you and your partner move the needle forward. If you don't do the work, you won't see the change. Truth. The tools are simple, but not always easy. They will help you to hold each other accountable to see real change and move forward in your relationship.

An important aspect of this journey is the spiritual one. A journey that Ryan and I strongly believe in and practice. That journey may not be the same one for you, right for you, or one you wish to develop at this stage in your life. I understand. However, there will be spirituality tips, tools, and stories woven into the fabric of this book. I intend to enlighten and share. I have had an innate knowing since I was a child, and only wish I had learned these tools and strengthened my intuition and knowing sooner in life. Ryan started at zero and has had an open mind as I have shared spiritual tools with him. I am grateful he is on board, but also realize that having an open mind to spiritual tools doesn't always happen in every relationship. If that ends up happening in yours, or sounds relatable to you on some level, again this book has served a purpose.

Thank you for joining me. Throughout this book, I am sharing stories and feelings which are deeply buried. Ryan and I have done the work, and continue to do so as new situations arise. (Note: it never ends). Bringing our experiences back to life is essential, because the stories and how we moved through the challenges are stories that can help others. I know this is cliché, but it's the truth: If we can do it, you can too.

If this helps one person and then that person helps another person....imagine what can be accomplished.

CHAPTER 1

Who the Heck Are We?

R ight now, you are probably wondering who we are and why you should listen to what we have to say about relationships. As I mentioned in the Intro, I am not a famous doctor who has traveled to China or India researching ancient secrets for years. As much as I respect and admire those people, I am confident in myself that sharing our real-life ordinary human experience is my role on this Earth. My husband Ryan and I are average people from middle-class families in Illinois.

Often, people can be intimidated by someone who has high credentials and has been a student of a modality (or several modalities) for many years. It creates the impression that, "Wow, I can't do that as I am not like him/her or never will be." That mindset isn't real; of course you can do it, too. When you realize that we are all one and that none of us is better than the other, you can achieve anything. You can move past your limiting beliefs. However, in reality, they still exist.

This book is full of a lot of information, tips, tools, and relatable stories, so you will find more than the average one nugget that the majority of people derive from a book; especially if you read between the lines.

Let the journey begin....

Ryan and I lost our high paying corporate jobs at the same time in 2009. Yep, the same time. Six months apart.

It was Christmas Eve, 2008. My boss was silently packing up her desk with the door closed. I saw the light under the door. She was supposed to be on vacation, so I was scratching my head, "What was going on?" I was a Senior Buyer with Shop NBC (now called Shop HQ) and we had already been through two rounds of layoffs in 2008. I knocked on her door. She ushered me into her office and told me to keep quiet. She was packing up her desk, and she advised me to do the same.

We were supposed to travel to NYC for the buying markets after the New Year. A few days prior, a memo had been sent cancelling our trip. I started packing my desk. She was right; 70 of us were let go shortly after the new year.

It was a mix of emotions. If you have ever been laid off or fired, you know. It's part relief, part shock *"Me? I'm awesome!"*, part scared out of your ever-loving mind, and of course such an event is a blow to your confidence.

Ryan and I had been manifesting moving to "somewhere it never snowed." He was suffering from depression, partly because of his unhappiness with his job as a plant supervisor, partly because we both weren't fans of living in snowy, cold Minneapolis, Minnesota (putting it nicely), and partly because we had a lot to work on individually and as a couple.

To move through the tough days, we would lay on top of the bed listening to ocean sounds on the sound machine. I would describe what it would be like when we moved somewhere where it never snowed. I had no idea what manifestation was, I just figured out that transporting him to a place of happiness helped with the pain of his daily situation.

Imagine the green grass all year round..... We have two Shih Tzus and can easily take them outside on walks.... You can go fishing any time you want and catch big fish like dolphin and wahoo..... You fish for a living and have your captain's license..... We own our own boat.... We see palm trees and sunshine every day.

Personally, I was also hell-bent on moving. I had envisioned living somewhere warm since I was a kid. Bing Crosby's Christmas song *Mele Kalikimaka* was burned into my brain. "*That's the island greeting that we send to you. From a land where palm trees swayed.*" I needed to make sure we were financially prepared, so in 2007, I started saying, "*if we cannot wear this in Florida, we cannot buy it.*" I didn't realize the impact of what I was speaking into existence. It became a game to me. I wasn't allowing us to buy any more winter coats, sweaters, boots, etc. *If we could not wear it in Florida, we could not buy it.* By the time we moved in 2009, both of our winter coats had holes in the armpits. No joke.

Being the take-action Type A planner that I am, I had assumed I would have a nice paying job as a buyer somewhere in the South (preferably Florida), and that company would move us. Once we were settled, Ryan would find a job doing something related to fishing, and then I would eventually move to a sales job, as I desired to be "pay for performance." This was the plan I was marching towards. What's the saying about best laid plans? The universe laughed. As I soon found out, it had another plan.

I was getting concerned and nervous that time was running out, and that my plan wasn't happening as I had desired. *Why wasn't my plan happening? What else should I be doing? Who should I be calling? Was I trying hard enough?* Looking for a new job was a full-time job in itself, and it was starting to eat at my thoughts as well as affect my positive mindset.

That May, I was home by myself, and in the midst of my feverish job search I decided to watch Oprah. She had a couple on her show talking about how they both lost their jobs at the same time. I sat there quietly, riveted, staring at the TV while the thoughts started to swirl. I knew intuitively that *that will be us. I need to brace myself now.* And my intuition was spot on. At 7 a.m. on June 6th, I received the call; Ryan was laid off, as well.

The day Ryan was laid off, we were fortunate to receive an invitation to go boating on Lake Minnetonka. We needed a break in energy, and it was obviously a rough morning. The invite came from a friend of a friend, as we didn't know the boat owner. It was indeed a lucky universe-driven event. We enjoyed a beautiful day on the water and had faith that the universe was figuring out our next steps, because when we started to think about our next steps, it was daunting.

So, the fact that I wouldn't buy us any new clothes starting in 2008 for the wintertime because, "We won't be able to wear that when we move to Florida," was pretty far out there to us. It was an out loud act of will and declaration towards our dreams, which I manifested. Our coats had several quarter sized holes in the arm-pits when I tossed them in the dumpster after the winter of 2009. With all of my determination, I declared, *We were not going to be in Minneapolis another winter.*

August 31, 2009, we left the parking garage of 110 W Grant Street and headed towards Florida with the final intention to land in The Keys. We didn't know a soul; we had no jobs, hardly any money, and we'd never even been to The Keys.

We started our journey to get on our feet as soon as we landed in The Florida Keys on October 1. I kept saying, *"Someday when we get our shit together we will help others."* Getting our shit together took many years, but we stayed positively persistent, had faith in the universe, and did the work.

Our vision, Good Karma Sportfishing, was launched January 1, 2012, and has only grown more successful with the passing years. The associated stories woven throughout this book are used as examples to help you build confidence in your relationship.

Helping you build that confidence and intimacy makes all of our challenges worthwhile.

CHAPTER 2

I Am Sooooo Pissed

"Melinda, what do you do if you are pissed off? Life can't be all happiness and rainbows."

I thought about adding a chapter on this topic. I had it on my chapter outline, but nothing was intuitively coming through to write. Truth be told, we are not perfect. I wanted the story to be real when I typed this chapter vs. a distant memory..... Well, ask and it is given. Funny, but not really, right?

I also wanted to have it at the beginning to set the stage that we are not perfect. I get tired of coaches acting like they have it all figured out. I don't, we don't, truth.

So here we go.... this morning....January 8, 2021.

Yep, I am pissed. Let me share first, have you ever created something that ends up snowballing and you wonder, *Should I have done this differently?* Those thoughts often have a lot of challenges in everything, from business to relationships to money. Reconsidering what actions or behaviors you have taken is a good part of learning and growing, otherwise you allow yourself to get stuck in the mud. And yes, "allow yourself" is true, because you own that.

I grew up watching my dad do so many things for my mom, and then he felt unappreciated. I could sense his feelings and awareness, and I realized the dynamics at a young age. Never think your children are not aware.

My mom barked orders all the time. At age 49, I can still hear her voice in my head, "Curt....." "Curt....."

Maybe that's why I have created the pattern Ryan and I live in now.

I do the laundry, cleaning, cooking, taking care of the dogs (the majority of the time), etc.; all are done by me. I live in fear of becoming my mother. So, my handling of household tasks is fine. I don't mind doing things, as I am not good at sitting still and I like to feel accomplished. Weird to say that taking out the garbage gives me a feeling of accomplishment, but it's true. *Is that a dopamine rush?*

If I ask he will help, but 75% of the time him helping is a result of me asking. And I strongly feel he is grateful, where I didn't feel I saw gratitude with my mother towards my father.

Do you go through this?

I find it amazing when a wife gushes on and on, telling me, "My husband does all the cooking and cleaning, and he is just amazing! I don't have to ask him anything, he just does it!"

Is she for real? Really? or is this an act? Maybe I can clone him....hmm.....

I know it's possible, but not in my household. I have worked on getting to a better place with some boundaries about what our house needs to look like when I get home from a trip, but it still isn't always perfect.

Progress over perfection. I have come to accept simple steps towards progress years ago. I celebrate progress as a win! I have also learned to monitor my thoughts, energy, words, behavior, expectations, you name it, but then there are times where those instances of not helping are too much....

Which is what happened this morning.

I woke up at my normal time of 4 a.m. and went about my daily routine. I made the coffee, then took two of the three dogs (Stella and Barena) out to go potty. Miracle (our third "child") likes to lounge around and is snippy if she is taken out too soon. What a princess!

One out of the two dogs poop, normally Stella, she is a good pooper. However, all three dogs need to go back into the kitchen until they have pooped, and then they can have breakfast. Yes, the dogs know this.

I checked my emails, FB, IG, LI, and then 4:40 a.m. had a mindset discussion with Ryan about dealing with the trolling motor on his boat. He has had to push through the terrible customer service we have received with this company for a year and a half. Yuck. Truly a yucky company; and it's been painful. I prayed to Archangel Michael the night before for a solution to this situation. I also prayed for it to work itself out easily.

I left for my walk at 5 a.m. and was back at 6 a.m. I showered and got ready for my day. My husband likes to leave clothes around in a few locations. You would think we have some amazing sex life where we tear each other's clothes off, and they end up all over the house like in the movies. Not.

So, the challenge is that I don't know if they are dirty because sometimes he tries things on and then leaves them somewhere. Like a girl would be doing while getting ready to go out on a date, but it's fishing t-shirts and shorts.

He was upstairs in our loft bedroom working on making lures for fishing when I went upstairs to get dressed.

"Hey Ryan, are these clothes on the bed dirty or clean?"

He snaps, "I don't know."

Hum....how the heck don't you know, right?

"How do you not know? You put them here."

Now, with a nasty tone and mocking me, he says, "I don't know!!!!"

Oh wow- you didn't really say that, did you?

"I am not a maid, and the dirty clothes bin is right here."

OMG! I am done.

No joke, the dirty clothes bin is an open basket within arm's length of the bed. It takes less than one ounce of energy to move clothes from the bed to the bin.

Seriously, WTF?!?!

I walked away. I could have stormed down the stairs, but that's not my style.

I went downstairs to meditate, closed the door, and said a prayer.

Dear God, Universe, Archangels, Spirit Tribe of the highest truth and compassion, my guardian angel and anyone else who wants to help me....Please help me not strangle my husband. Amen. Is it done.

During my meditation, it came to me to write this chapter for the book on being pissed.

Thanks team!

As I said in the intro, I am not a psychiatrist or someone who has traveled all over China for 30 years meditating with monks. I am an average person who has average shitty things happen, and those things affect my energy.

It is our main job to stay on the positive energy tracks. It seems simple, but it's not.

I cannot control him to make him put the clothes away. I am not a maid. I do not deserve to be spoken to rudely. And heck, it's clothes to be put in a bin. Again, seriously, WTF?!

During my meditation, I also made a pact with myself; I was done with him for the day unless he apologized on his own. I have a few friends that go for days without speaking to their husbands. I have never been that way, but this was a strong option as my mind was reeling from the laundry bin incident.

I had already made Ryan his breakfast, refilled his coffee, filled his water glass, and put his vitamins out. I know many women (or men) that would say, "Seriously?" Yes, I do this. I own it, and 9.9 times out of 10, it's fine, and I don't mind at all. Again, it goes back to not wanting to be like my mom, barking orders, so I take care of it myself.

Today it was not fine. I was this close to tossing Ryan's breakfast in the garbage, but I don't like to waste food. I grew up hearing, "Eat your dinner. There are starving kids in Africa." So, I am not wasteful. But when does it stop?

I took Miracle (our third dog) out for her walk. I told her point-blank, "Your dad is an asshole." She and I have never had that discussion before. Miracle kept trotting her cute little self down the street, oblivious to anything but her own need to poop so she could finally eat breakfast.

Mission accomplished. I headed back inside, fed the dogs, and held my breath.

Am I going to have to ignore Ryan all day? Does he get it? I don't have time for this bad energy or behavior.

Luckily, to my surprise, kinda like, "When what to my wondering eyes did appear" out of the scene from *'Twas the Night Before Christmas,* Ryan came downstairs and apologized.

It was a simple, "I'm sorry." We hugged and moved on. I am not the type of person who rehashes and keeps the fight going. I am happy with an apology, an acknowledgment, and forward positive movement. Over the years, I have witnessed couples who keep the fight going. If this is happening in your relationship, stop and take note now.

A few days later, after I shared my initial draft of this chapter, he proceeded to talk more about the incident. I hadn't realized that my behavior had shifted since I started drinking coffee. I started drinking coffee in July when I started a weight loss/healthy lifestyle program. I was drinking coffee in lieu of Diet Coke. I used to drink a lot of Diet Coke, and I made it a goal in July to cut back. This was the first time in my life that I started drinking coffee, so it was a new adventure.

He calls the intensity folks get from too much coffee, "coffee rage," because he sometimes has it, too. My energy is above normal to begin with. So, imagine that after a few cups of coffee, and then my morning power walk, I have even more energy than he does. He is a morning person in the sense that he gets up early, however it takes him awhile to adjust to the day. I wake up with my "brain on fire," ready to go! The discussion about the difference in our energy level first thing in the morning has gone on for years. Nowadays, in the first hour when he gets up, I always ask, "Are you ready to talk?" before I open my mouth and start spewing thoughts and ideas. However, this clothing bin incident was several hours after we woke up, so my high energy shouldn't have been an issue.

Ryan was trying to get something done; he was focused and extremely frustrated because he wanted to go fishing. He had a booked charter, and the weather in the Florida Keys had been a nightmare for months. The weather has been the worst we have ever witnessed in our 11 years living here. It would be depressing to count how many trips have been canceled or rescheduled, and there is nothing we can do about it. We made it a pact to hunker down, stay positive, and deal.

I interrupted his focus along with his internal stewing; hence the cold (more like icy) snap.

Brrr...I should have dressed warmer to venture upstairs.

Later on, I asked him, "Why didn't you tell me sooner about the coffee hype?"

His answer, "I didn't want to cause any confusion or drama."

About me being amped up on coffee? Really?

This is where a lot of couples, and people in general, struggle. As a normal human, I don't see how it would cause any drama by telling me I am a bit much to take after a cup of coffee with a top off. But, people have a fear of what **could** happen. What **could** become an argument from a simple thing, such as a shirt not being tossed in the bin and Ryan having a bad morning. A story created in their head. And, may I add, when he told his story, I pictured myself as a raving coffee head lunatic, which is certainly not the case. What story do you create in your head?

CONFIDENCE MASTERY FOR COUPLES

"Next time," I said to Ryan, "Please tell me sooner about any changes in my behavior, because I wasn't aware. And I am open to listening to your feedback. Please!"

Whew! I can get on with my day and not have to deal with negative energy. Thank you! Thank you! Thank you!

Do I have some secret sauce to have had this happen, and Ryan apologizing? I don't know, exactly. My prayer for help likely contributed, as I believe in the divine. That is in conjunction with the many years of going through all of the things I will be sharing in this book AND doing the work. Maybe now that I think of it, the combination is the secret sauce.

But now...days later.... it gets better. *Hmm....I wish I could say "juicier" but that's not the case.*

I thought the case was closed. I had given some chapters to some fellow authors who I admire for their honest feedback. One friend sent feedback to me regarding some points in this story. It took me a second to get grounded, as I wasn't prepared for what she had to say. It seemed off base to me, but then again, it was her perception, which I respected. My intuition was telling me something was amiss. I moved through those feelings and decided to reread what I wrote to Ryan along with her email.

Ryan's look was puzzling, "No, I don't think you have a coffee caffeine problem at all. It was my fault that I spoke to you in that way to begin with. My frustration with the charter being canceled was what prompted my response."

What? Another layer! Another layer of realization, thoughts, and communication. We all have them. We think more about a situation, often letting time pass, and things start to settle a bit. You calm down and your mind can clear. Initially, his feedback was my energy level and I owned it. I added his thoughts to the chapter. But then it didn't make 100% sense to me, because I am high energy and it's not that much coffee. Upon further discussion, he went back and owned his initial snap.

THIS layer of connection and story is what I want you to understand as you read this. We are all complicated human beings and we don't always get it right the first time or even the second time.

Our communication wasn't perfect. There were a few instances that could have been avoided. We could have had better communication about his emotions, my high-energy morning/coffee vibe, and what he was working on upstairs. We are all a work in progress.

I will also add confidence to keep going and accept the feedback, communication as a tool, and compassion all get credit from an energy level. Our goal was to push through the situation with as minimal bad energy as possible. We did not continue the argument.

Screaming, yelling, stomping off, and anything else along this line of behavior don't work. It doesn't solve the issue of fixing challenges; you may have to work on yourself or as a couple.

As I said in my intro, Ryan is an amazing guy. I love him with all my heart and know we are meant to be. However, we all have moments that are rough: bad days, trying times, stress, AND for some icing, Covid-19. It's how we handle the challenges that define us.

Begin and see the positive change.

Now, let's begin.

CHAPTER 3

Are You Trying to Change Me?

No Glass Houses

An old European saying states, "Those who live in glass houses should not throw stones." I have always used that saying to remind myself that not everyone is perfect, including me. Therefore, don't judge others or be too hard on yourself.

With a kind spirit and grace, I will ask you to take a look at yourself first as you consider the two questions below. This step is crucial in understanding how you approach people, relationships, and life. If you and your partner can do this individually, your change and growth will be that much faster.

Again, you must work on yourself first.

Think about:

1. Are you trying to change the other person?
2. Are you aware of what you should change to help the situation?

I remember when I was dating a guy named Jim way back when I lived in Columbus, Ohio. My parents noticed my intense need to control him and called me out. The four of us were waiting to go into a restaurant and I took charge of getting the table, like I would normally do. My mother made some snide comment like, "Have to take control again." To be honest, being called out was shocking, and it stung. Her tone always had a pierce to it, and I felt embarrassed. *"I was only trying to get a table and she embarrassed me in front of the guy I like."* However, it was the first time I had been made aware of my controlling nature, and at 27 years old, it was eye-opening. My thoughts started to swirl, *"Where did this stem from and is this affecting my relationships?"*

Years went by, and I still found myself taking control. One relationship after another, I tried to change the other person. This was also a theme for me in work relationships and with associates on my team. I was naive to think everyone desired the same goals as me. *"Doesn't everyone want to be a CEO?"*

Then one day, something amazing happened when I was a merchant for Victoria's Secret. Have you ever taken a personality test? There are many options available. I remember taking the Herman Brain Dominance Indicator (HBDI) along with my team to see what color and skillset we were. The color coding showed our strengths. It was eye-opening. I was not getting along with one of the planners on my team and his color was blue. I was frustrated with him, which affected my energy and our working relationship.

After taking HBDI, I learned that his blue skill set meant he was strong in math. I was yellow, which shows creativity. Allowing him to build upon his strength in numbers, even showcasing it and delegating projects that he liked, allowed him to excel, strengthen the team overall, and set the relationship on a better path. Quite frankly, it also took projects that were not my strength or passion off my plate so I could focus on what I did enjoy. It ended up being a win-win.

The test was eye-opening. It led me to a new awareness that everyone was different, which was okay. I learned it was fun to encourage different skill sets. Yes, encouraged, because it balanced out the team.

I learned something very important that day: appreciate your similarities but also respect your differences.

Encouraging people's differences may seem like common sense, but people don't apply the thought process. Think about politics. The premise of our system is to be balanced. If everyone thought the same way and had the same beliefs, change wouldn't happen, and progress as we know it wouldn't exist. So why is there such negatively-charged energy around someone who has a different point of view?

Most people fall into the trap of trying to change someone. And most people don't realize it. I will say this repeatedly, because it's worth repeating so it sticks; most people live on autopilot. When you make a conscious effort to get off of autopilot, you will see your life start to change, evolve, and one could hope, become better. But, if you don't it stays the same. If you read this book and don't put any of the tips or stories into practice, your life will not change.

"Who the 'f' was I to try to change someone?"

The relationship I was in before my husband Ryan was a nightmare. From start to finish. But it was a clear example of trying to change someone that couldn't be changed. Better put, he didn't want to change. And who was I to think that I could do that? I went through all the steps; counseling, help from parents, even Al-Anon, but nothing worked, and I had to walk away. That decision was tough and took time and guidance from the universe, but in the end made sense. Today I am grateful.

"Why am I still not learning my lesson? What is wrong with me?"
You may be scratching your head by now. You would think I would
have learned my lesson heading into my relationship with Ryan.
But I didn't learn my lesson. However, he wanted to change, and I
did, too. I feel that I got very lucky. But, I worked on myself first.
So, after that major falling out, standing in our kitchen, the change
started. We decided to figure it out.

What drove me so fiercely was the thought of another failed
relationship. And obviously, I was starting to put the pieces together
of where my behavior stemmed from and was hell-bent to change
it. My parent's relationship (now divorced) was not a role model
marriage example. As far back as I remember, it was like screeching nails on a chalkboard feeling when I noticed how my mother
controlled situations and how my father went along, even though I
could sense he wasn't happy. I could feel it in my bones. And here I
was doing the same thing. I needed to stop operating on autopilot,
take the learnings that I recognized, and apply them to my own
life. Hence, stop judging others when I had the same issues. No
glass houses.

Here's the thing. When you are pushing against something, it
doesn't feel good, right? Often, we live in stress, talk to our friends
about it, think about it all day long, and all of that makes it worse.
You are not releasing anything if you do not recognize the challenges
you own and then communicate about it with your spouse.

There is a point where you can laugh at your weaknesses. Some
people refer to weaknesses as gifts. I don't disagree with looking at it
that way. It helps alleviate any self-judgment you may have or think
others may be judging you for.

It'll be five years this March that Ryan gave up drinking. We
were the typical social drinkers. Some embarrassing drunken stories
here and there that we would like to forget or better yet, pretend
they didn't happen. But, one day he felt it was finally time to call
it quits. We were going out to dinner, and instead of his usual cold
beer, he ordered a Diet Coke. I about fell off my chair. I was speech-

less. You realize someone gets it when they stop cold turkey on their own. He understood the power of change and did it. Not "tried to" but "did it".

Was quitting regular social drinking easy for him? No. I assumed it was because of drunk drivers in conjunction with people's behaviors in The Keys. "The Keys Disease" is a real thing. People move down here and are easily sucked into the party scene- drinking and drugs. We have witnessed people's health deteriorate. We also witnessed our former neighbor tragically die after she went down an alcoholic and pill popping lifestyle. But, in his honesty and transparency, he quit because he wanted to be better for our relationship.

A few years after we met, I realized that rum was "the devil." And it was. I noticed the pattern of when he drank rum, his demeanor would change. Beer wasn't as bad, but it became unnecessary. A lot of captains down here also have drinking problems and are known to have reputations of hanging around the marina drinking after a charter. He wanted a different life.

Shortly thereafter, Ryan inspired me to have the confidence to quit my regular evening glass of wine. Well, let's be honest, it was more than one glass. My reasoning was also to feel better, but in addition, cut some unnecessary calories. I thought for years, *No way can I give up my evening glass of wine! I fricking deserve this. I work hard, deal with crap all day. This is my treat.*

Do you just say something like that in your head, too? There is power in both parties deciding to make a change and inspiring each other without force. We ended up changing together which is also an important part of staying together.

Once you start to see this in action and realize it's possible, you can build momentum for other shifts, as well. And I wanted to see if I could do it—*heck if he could do it why couldn't I?*

"Thank you Ryan."

If you only say one prayer in a day, make it Thank You.- Rumi

One of the bravest parts of developing your confidence is recognizing that you need to change and you may need help. Help can come from you recognizing the need for change on your own, through your partner, or a third party. Moving past your ego so you can change plays a big part, as well. Our ego is there to keep us safe, but often it can do more harm than good when we let it rule us. Our ego doesn't want to ask for help. It thinks it knows everything and is perfect. We are perfect in a sense; however, we still have imperfections which, when mastered, become our gifts.

Work on yourself first and get to a place of happiness on a consistent basis. This will build your confidence. As a result, manifesting your dreams, personally or as a couple, will be a closer reality.

CHAPTER 4

The Big Scary Word - Intentions

"Our intention creates our reality." —Wayne Dyer

If you are like me, you have likely heard it before.

What is Your Why? What is your intention? What is your pur-pose? Why are you doing this? Why do you *do things?*

Have you heard these questions before? Have you taken action or ignored them?

This is serious business, so here are some things to think about:

1. What is your biggest dream or goal?
2. Why do you want to achieve it?

Now ask your partner the same questions. Are you both on the same page? Your intentions can work hand and hand with your actions and develop your roadmap in life. If you are not on the same page, it can be frustrating, challenging, misleading, and worse, you can fall out of love.

That's what we are going to chat about in this chapter. Couples being on the same page.

People ask me why do I coach, speak, and write about confidence? Here is why: look around you, listen, read; the word confidence is used for so many aspects of your daily life and goals. It's tossed around like a hot potato, but is easily dropped and squashed. Confidence is a pillar; a foundation for which you can build your life.

Two other pillars are communication and compassion. All of them important and work with each other.

How many of you can honestly say that you and your partner are on the same page 100% of the time? Daily life? Goals and dreams? If you are, kudos! But, most are not. What's been interesting over the years, because Ryan and I are child-free, we notice that often couples aren't even on the same page about having children. They haven't even discussed it. The decision to have children and how many children to have is beyond important because it's a life. And I have been privy to countless conversations in which the topic to have or not have children has never been discussed.

Years ago, Ryan and I went to a friend's beach house for a long relaxing weekend. The couple was child-free and in their late 30s. She (let's call her Angelique) was so consumed with herself she never realized her husband (let's call him Connor) wanted children.

Connor's desire for children reflected in his brown eyes. When we were out and about on the town and he saw children, his eyes lit up. When he spoke about his nieces and nephews you could tell it was with heartfelt longing. Angelique would dominate the conversation so fiercely that Connor never got a word in. I don't think they ever discussed having children. Do you see yourselves in them?

Regarding our decision to be child-free, one of the most serious conversations a couple can have, happened while holding our metal Bud Light beer cans high so folks nearby splashing around wouldn't get water in our beer. We were standing in a crowded pool at the Mirage Hotel in Las Vegas on a hot August day. Vegas was fun, but seriously, great timing for a conversation about children?

To dial this back, I had lost my brother, Bryan, a few years earlier due to blood clots. He tragically fell over and died. When he passed away, we were not aware of the reason. It took a few months before the autopsy came back. My parents were advised to have their daughters (me and my sister Debra) tested for the gene, as it would not be wise to try to have a child if the issue was present. I have low protein S, my sister is fine. Learning I was low protein S was a sign, as I had not felt a motherly urge like my sister did. Now, how do you tell this to the guy you are madly in love with and think you will marry? The conversation plagued me. Even though there are millions of child-free couples, it is still more common to have children, and often expected. My mind was often flooded with worry and anxiety about having the conversation. *Will he break up with me? Will he feel like he is settling? Will this always haunt our relationship? Will I be perceived like Angelique?*

So how did the conversation come about? Ryan randomly blurted out, "You should probably know I don't want to have kids." Wow. I stood there speechless but also relieved. And just like that, it was settled. A heavy weight was lifted off me. Prior to the beer-laden enlightenment, I struggled thinking, *Was I a bad woman for not desiring to have children? Was I selfish? Was something wrong with me?*

After that point, I realized getting the cat out of the bag about whatever you desire or intend in life is crucial. The mind loops that can occur when you haven't discussed your hopes, dreams, and wishes with your partner can become overbearing and consuming. Anxiety can be a heavy burden and wreck havoc not only on your mindset, but also on your body and health. The elephant in the room should always be addressed but often isn't. And here, Ryan and I were on the same page all along.

Have the discussion.

Take time to sit down and go over your goals and dreams.

To do this, plan a date night. And remember these essential skills that may seem simple, but are not easy: breathe, pause, really listen, and take your time. If you have a hard time remembering to breathe, pause, listen, and take your time, write those words on a sticky note and have it with you. Remember, you are not alone. We all can get caught up in interrupting, trying to get the last word in, not listening, etc. I am often guilty, hence how I know to call it out.

Years ago, when I was in the corporate world, I had an extremely supportive boss. Every time I came to him with a challenge, before I was done telling the story he would pick up the phone to try to help. I realized that sometimes I didn't need help. I just needed to get "it" out, i.e. vent. I remember asking so clearly, thanking my boss for being supportive but also kindly letting him know that I didn't always need help; I needed to share. We came to an agreement, which was that before I started to tell him what was wrong, I would say, *"I am just letting you know this, and I am not expecting or needing any assistance. I just need to tell you this."* That communication strategy was helpful. I felt that he became very "Papa Bear" in protecting his team. I was grateful, but it could be overbearing.

I find that I do the same thing with Ryan. I quickly jump into Mama Bear mode instead of listening and taking a moment before reacting. Since that isn't helpful and often puts us into a bigger spin with a lot of negative energy, I have adopted this tactic with Ryan in our relationship.

However, in full transparency, sometimes we fall off the wagon and need a reminder. Writing this chapter is my reminder, as I fell off the other day. It happens. Our most common Mama Bear scenario is when Ryan has a challenging client. He works hard and is so talented that my fierce sharp claws come out. You don't want to meet me in a dark forest when my Mama Bear alter ego comes out. I have worked hard to recognize it. When this happens and I jump into Mama Bear mode, I need to stop myself or have him stop me.

Progress over perfection, right? Keep this in mind as you go through these discussions that yes, you will fall off the wagon, but do your best to course correct, apologize, get back up, and do better next time.

CHAPTER 5

The "C" Word -
Communication

"Sometimes one creates a dynamic impression by saying something, and sometimes one creates as significant an impression by remaining silent."
—The Dalai Lama

*A*nd I just stared at him in silence......thinking about what to say next in the best way possible. Without tone, and being cautious to say the right thing the right way.
I wish I could say I do this all the time. Do you?

1. Are you good at being silent and listening? Focused listening, not playing with your phone?
2. Is your partner focused on listening to you when you talk?

How does it happen that we know the right way to be, but don't always do it. As I sit here on December 27th writing this book, gazing out my window...it's a bright sunny 60 degrees in The Keys, which is freezing. I know; poor me, right? When it gets this cold, iguanas freeze and fall out of trees. People have been known to bring their grills inside to keep warm (definitely not a bright idea). And my husband is on his way home from a fishing charter. I know how it went. I know the client. I know the weather was harsh and the client has big expectations which can wear on my husband. However, I know he slayed the fish and am quite sure his client is over the moon happy. But, what will he say when he walks in the door, and how will I react?

A lot of books are written on communication. People specialize in communication; coaches, therapists, teachers, etc. Why? Because it is one of the most essential tools you can master. Mastering communication leads you down a path of success in everything. Business tactics such as advertising need strong copy. Getting things done or delegating requires communication. And relationships require communication to exist and grow.

One of my favorite movies that we watch every holiday is *Love Actually*. Ryan tries to deny that he likes the movie, but then he gets into it, remembering the character Colin and his wild time in Wisconsin, which ironically is where Ryan used to live. Ryan only wishes he got to sleep naked with four hot chicks. The story between Jamie and Aurelia is my favorite plotline. Not only because he is a writer and living my dream of writing a novel in a rented cottage in France, but the communication which ensues first non-verbally, but then grows when they learn each other's language is full of depth. They learn to understand each other without speaking. Again, silence.

Communication is a learning, just like relationships are a lesson. You try, you fail, you pick yourself back up, and once in awhile, you may give yourself a high five for handling it well.

"The quieter you become, the more you are able to hear." – Rumi

Rumi was a 13th century Persian poet. Stop and think about that. The same stuff was said in the 13th century and likely even earlier, and we are still talking and writing about it now.

I had breakfast with two friends today; one is a published author and the other is a marketing expert and coach. We ended up having this discussion as they were sharing some tools and ideas with me. Tools may change with time and advancement, i.e. technology, social media. But the thought processes, methodologies, and overall lessons remain the same. Quotes by well known historical figures such as Rumi, Mark Twain, Eleanor Roosevelt, and Albert Einstein remain valid and impactful many years later.

How do we not learn and change?

As coaches, we are taught to ask open-ended questions, feeling questions, and work toward understanding the other person. Using questions that primarily begin with What vs Why are helpful in softening the tone and working towards a solution.

Examples- you and your partner are on vacation, and you take a wrong turn which puts you behind schedule to meet your family for lunch. You ask:

Good example: "What led you to decide to head north on 95 vs south?"

Bad example: "Why did you do that?"

These are simple examples can be easily applied if you took a moment to stop and think before speaking.

So, let's circle back to Ryan coming home from his charter. Since my brain started firing on all communication cylinders, it would be pathetic if I f-ed this up, right? Well, good news! I didn't. I was calm, listened, and to my surprise, he shared details that were positive and overall (sans the rough weather) it was a great day. I do believe our conversation goes down in the books as a win. He has worked on being positive when he walks in the door, and I was relaxed and calm, ready to handle whatever came my way without being Mama Bear. We've come a long way! But keep in mind, as mentioned before, the work is never finished.

When you work on communication as a couple (or in any relationship), honesty and feedback are crucial. Circling back to the story I shared in the intro, I don't know if the feedback about my tone in relation to my mother could have been any more honest. It was direct and maybe not the best advised delivery; however, as I mentioned, I needed to hear it, so I was open. It was time.

There's a little feedback trick I had learned years ago in the corporate world (one of the many trainings I sat through) that often works magic. The magic trick is to ask the other person what it is about themselves that you may have a challenge with. Let me give you an example:

> "Ryan, what's something that Melinda would say bugs her about you?"

> "Melinda, what's something that Ryan would say bugs him about you?"

It's a simple question-answer series that is enlightening. Often, one says what the other is thinking. That realization can even lead to laughter as they realize they are on the same wave-length. Make this discussion part of your date night.

What do you do if the other person doesn't want to participate? I am smiling as I type this, as I have been there many times before. It's not always the easiest task to get a discussion going. I work on it over time. Something I have found to be very helpful is to get a third party's (or outsider's) viewpoint or suggestion. What does this mean? There are many times when Ryan doesn't want to listen to me. Or, it's about something I have discussed with him a million times before (exaggerating but you get my point). I feel like I am beating my head against a brick wall. I try to see myself as him and understand why he isn't listening or doesn't understand. However, It can be extremely exhausting and wear on my nerves. I aim to stay on my positive railroad tracks, so when he is off it affects me.

What ends up happening, to my delight, is that I come across some content in which the author, spiritual teacher, coach, or speaker is discussing the very thing I have been trying to communicate.

Genius! Let them do the work. I am totally fine with delegating! Why not free up some of my energy?

The next step is to get your partner to listen and digest the information, which may also take work or some time, but is possible. Keep going! Eventually with a little help from the universe (especially if you ask/pray for help), the message will eventually be relayed, and not surprisingly, when it doesn't come from you, often your partner may be more open to receiving.

Score!

Now, here's my big struggle. The "I know." I am working hard to keep my energy neutral as I type this.

Keep calm, Melinda, keep calm, breathe...

The "I know, leave me alone," struggle can be the most grating. Often, it can lead people down a war path. I work hard to keep my calm. Meditation is a huge help. Oh, yeah, meditation is one of those, "I know" topics. He knows he should be meditating daily, but he doesn't. There you have it. Full circle, right?

Addressing the "I knows" but not the "I am doing" isn't my favorite fun conversation spot. Like I have said before, if I had a nickel...I will admit, the fact that Ryan chooses to say, "I know" vs. actually doing a good portion of time is a work in progress. In addition, his tone and delivery can come out quite defensive. Do you see this in yourself or your partner? It's not uncommon for someone to say, "I know, leave me alone." Or "I get it!" Celebrate when one of you does truly get it, and this becomes an old story you can laugh at.

Again, the work never ends. Don't give up and don't lose faith! You are not alone.

CHAPTER 6

Reframing and Triggers

"From now on, I want you to practice reframing other people's negativity as a reminder of a way not to be."—T Harv Eker

This next chapter's lesson is one in which you will get the hang of and it will become second nature, but like anything, it takes practice.

Reframing. Have you heard of it before? If so, do you practice it? Or should I ask, do it?

Reframing is the key to changing your mindset and communication with others. It's the same as changing the plot in a movie or TV show. You catch it, stop it ("it" being the thought or comment), and reword or rethink it. Mastering the art of reframing is life changing and the key to shifting your mindset. You are changing your mental picture.

1. When I have a negative thought, do I let it flow by? Say it out loud to my partner? Or think it over and over?
2. If I notice my partner saying something negative, do I stop him/her?

You can read about reframing all day long, but until you put it into motion, it doesn't mean diddly squat. I also highly recommend doing the exercises that I will mention in this chapter and finding a way to help keep each other accountable or hire a coach. It's crucial to do the work in this section to catch yourself or your partner when negative thoughts arise and experience the change that reframing can bring.

Find an emotionless safe code word.

Sounds a little S&M, so it will make you laugh as you say it and break the energy.

If you can say "reframe" that's great, if not no worries, find another word. Words can be along the lines of - cotton candy, vacation, sunshine. Something fun that you both agree to say when you feel you need to reframe. It may be cheesy, but sometimes that helps you to remember it. And what's wrong with laughing at the cheesy stuff in life?

The key to reframing is not only to change your mindset and communication, but also to shift the energy behind your words. All of these aspects feed into your subconscious mind. When the two of you are on the same page with challenges, dreams, visions, goals, desires, health, etc. the magic can happen faster, and you can support each other emotionally. There is a lot packed into that sentence. Reread it and make sure it sinks in. If you can master reframing, you are on the road to success.

Now on to some examples in our household:

I am sure you would agree that heavy lifting is easier with a partner. Imagine trying to get your old couch out the front door all by yourself while your partner is sitting in the kitchen eating chips. Wait a second...*I think I am describing my world; anyhow...* When one person does all the heavy lifting themselves, they get worn out tired, hurt, and don't move as fast. It's the same analogy with communication and mindset shifts. If you both can be working towards the same goals and calling each other out when something that is said is out of sync or alignment, think how much faster you will get the big piece of furniture out the door. Why not help each other with reframing and shifting your mindset?

We go through this exchange regularly, as there is always something that comes up which can be viewed negatively, but positively shifted.

Bonus thought to sink in- Some shift examples may seem far-fetched, but if you believe in manifestation, you will start to understand how this works.

Example- Ryan and one of his fishing friends were chatting, and his friends said to him, "You are going to be slammed with other boats this weekend. I am off to the Bahamas."

Where does your mind go first? Over the years, a statement like this would send Ryan into a competitive tailspin. "Oh no, that many boats? It's going to be a mess. They are going to be on my spots and I won't be able to catch any fish for my clients."

Ryan would get frustrated and start thinking about how crowded it would be on the water, with boats cutting him off and overall rudeness.

This loop would send me into a Mama Bear tailspin, talking about taking out his camera phone or being upset that he went down a negative path so quickly. The energy created by both of us would be unpalpable, unnecessary energy, which didn't serve either of us.

When he first told me about what his friend said, I have to admit, I did brace myself. *Oh no, here we go!*

However, I was proudly and presently surprised. The practice has created change! Instead of the usual negative pattern and spin, he said to me, "I am looking forward to when I head off to the Bahamas, too."

Wow! I think I am going to fall over. My brain whirled as I pinched myself. Done. No bad energy, no bad spin.

Remember The Law Of Attraction? Keep that in mind as you go through your reframing. What you think about and talk about, especially out loud, comes true. With that thought process and practice, I am planning what I am going to wear when I go along to the Bahamas with him. Likely I will be by the pool or at the beach vs. fishing, but he can go fishing!

Another reframing that can come in handy is when you feel that little green monster creep up. Admit it, the green monster happens to everyone at some point or another. This specific example I am about to give will also help with negative beliefs you may have from childhood, when your parents may have said something like, "Keep dreaming, kid." Or "Only rich people can afford a boat." Sound familiar? Sometimes we wonder where jealousy and envy come from, and it may be buried from when you were a kid and told you couldn't have something.

A specific reframe example for me relates to something I desire; a jet ski. When I see a jet ski, instead of saying things such as, "How did they afford that?" I switch to, "I am super excited to own a jet ski someday!" Shifting your mindset and reframing your dialogue all contributes to better energy, as well as conversations with others.

Taking a Step Back and Breaking it Down

Amid the cleaning frenzy I was guided to do, I discovered a journal from 2009, when Ryan and I were newly married.

Can you guess what I journaled about back then? The same shit. Yep, the same mindset behavior, just packaged a bit differently. The tangible goals, like him catching a big wahoo, having a fishing captain's license, and moving somewhere where it never snowed had been achieved, but the mindset goals were still a work in progress. Of course, the work never ends because even if you have perfected your mindset, you still have to maintain. Same as working out or losing weight; you have to maintain and continue to do the reps. I am proud to say that there has been improvement. But, there is still work to be done.

The example of finding my old journal is one of the main reasons I wanted to write this book. Change takes work. You have to put in the work to see change and progress. Writing down your thoughts and ideas in a nice pretty journal and then putting it on your shelf doesn't help you or your spouse. I am all for the pretty journals, I have a stack, but a legal pad would also work just fine.

Whether You Want to Admit it or Not - We All Have Triggers

The discussion that happened after I found the journal was enlightening and intense at the same time. It's frustrating when you, yet again, discuss the same patterns that are appearing over and over. You would be a lunatic if you disagreed. What's that saying by Albert Einstein?

"Insanity is repeating the same thing over and over and expecting different results."

And when was Albert Einstein alive? Early 1900's. I think you get my point.

We are finally at a place of understanding triggers and openly discussing them. This is a huge milestone.

When you start to discuss triggers from an open and honest place, you can move forward. Triggers can be embarrassing for some people. Let's face it, envy, which is a huge trigger, isn't something folks openly admit to. Who comes out and says, "I am jealous of my neighbor's car," and makes it a discussion?

Our challenges repeatedly are caused by the fact that I am an over thinker who can go into Mama Bear overdrive very quickly. Ryan over analyzes people and often lets it affect his mood.

How does this play out and contribute to a massive head loop that results in bad energy? Let me walk you through...

Ryan, "I can't believe he called me again to ask about the weather and also increased to five people. He knows I don't take five people and the weather is the weather. What should I say to him?"

Me, "Ryan, we've discussed this a million times before....." and then I feel my frustration rise. I can feel the blood start to pulse, and my tone, which I inherited from my mother, starts to comes out. I have to stop. Or, let me put it this way, I have learned that I need to stop. It's hard to describe tone in a book, but think of someone who rubs you the wrong way, and no matter what you can feel the negative energy in your skin. And often, when you break down the actual words that they said, the words aren't that bad, it's likely the tone that was off-putting.

Tone can be more damaging than most realize. It sticks in your head and can replay like a bad song you wish to turn off on the radio, but you can't get to the dial fast enough.

Now I do my best (not always perfect- progress over perfection) to not have a tone or to catch it immediately. My dialogue back to Ryan has shifted to, "That's nice they want to book a charter with you. What are you going to tell them?"

I helped the situation by shifting it to a positive and softening my tone. My shift stops Ryan in his tracks if he were going to go down a negative path. He may not be happy or agree with the point of view I take. However, it is a track stopper. The shift stops him and causes him to think first and then reframe.

Keep this story in mind to reflect on and remember as you go about your day and conversations.

Transformation lies in reframing.

CHAPTER 7

Energy in Everything

"All the breaks you need in life wait within your imagination. Imagination is the workshop of your mind capable of turning mind energy into accomplishment and wealth." —Napoleon Hill.

E nergy is everywhere; in every tangible thing AND every thought, emotion, cell, and action. Your body exudes energy as much as, let's say, the pen you are using to write in your journal as you take notes reading this book- hint hint.

I aimed to find a way to help others understand that energy is all around us, and we are energy. Since it's not necessarily the most tangible concept, it can be confusing and grey. In *The Good Karma Success Coach Podcast* Episode 108, returning guests Dr. Isabel Perez and Dr. Jyun help break it down by relating that we all have infinite (aka quantum) potential.

I could go down a more scientific or intense spiritual path of discussing energy, but I wish to keep this book in relatable examples that anyone can easily pick up and apply. I am not heavy into science, and there are plenty of resources available both scientifically and spiritually for you to consume if you are interested in learning more.

When someone says the word "energy" to you, what do you think?

Are you aware of your energy or your partner's energy? Because without understanding your energy, how it relates to others, and especially how it relates to your partner, nothing can be fully accomplished.

I remember when I first started as a sales rep. Stores would say to me, "You are a ray of sunshine, you have such positive energy." I think those statements were my first realization about energy and how I affect others. On the flip side, as I got to know my customers better, they would share stories with me about other sales reps, and I related how they felt to their energy.

Many quotes you read or hear relate to this thought process, but not many people understand, share, or practice what it means. Hence, there is a vast disconnect not only within a single person but within a couple.

Here are some excellent examples:

> "Miracles start to happen when you give as much energy to your dreams as to your fears." —Price Ea

> "Don't use your energy to worry, use your energy to believe."—Unknown?

> "If you want to attract positive things into your life. Then begin by spreading positive energy about." —Lynda Field

"Be the energy you want to attract."—Unknown

"Positive Vibes."

All these quotes are excellent, but it's not about the quote. It's about understanding the core of the passage and how to apply it daily to get results. I see people posting quotes on Facebook that do not practice what they preach. By that I mean the actual energetic feeling you get when having positive thoughts and posting positive sayings, but acting negatively or posting about other subjects that don't often have positives thoughts attached. A good example is politics or other topics that could trigger someone.

Triggers and Energy

"Your main job is to be positive or at least be neutral."

I have heard it said many times before and have had it spoken to me in readings as a direction from my guides.

And yes, I say it to Ryan.

I do my best to live this 'job' every day, but it takes work. After having the cause and effect of how we use our energy etched into my brain so it's second nature, the next part of the work is recognizing our triggers and stopping them.

Here are two examples from 2020, in which I had to take time to recognize my triggers and work on stopping them at the door.

My three cute little Shih Tzus are triggering. "What? Dogs are supposed to be the happiest part of your day!"

Sure, you have heard the saying, "Sorry, I like my dogs more than most humans." Yes, you may think I am a wacko or a mean person. Maybe even a terrible person. But it's true; my dogs have been a trigger for me for quite some time. That doesn't mean I don't love them or would ever hurt them. But sometimes I wish they'd take care of themselves or take a vacation.

When I was in coaching class, part of our curriculum was to coach each other. The topic had to be authentic, not pretend. After several weeks, I struggled with ideas because I felt I had covered everything to date; my husband, my current sales job, people, and my weight, which was always a looming topic. But we hadn't yet discussed my dogs and the guilt I felt about keeping them in the kitchen all day while I was home working.

My three little dogs are a trigger. They were often sending me down a path of anxiety and (gasp!) even anger if they misbehaved. They each have different personalities and can be a handful. And finding pee in the living room when they have been potty trained for years is never fun. It would set me off on a downward spiral, and I felt ashamed because they are loving creatures who don't mean any intentional harm.

I was always afraid to speak up about my dogs and how I felt because of the judgment. Fear of judgment is one of the most paralyzing challenges one must face and conquer to move forward. What kind of person doesn't love animals? *What was I dealing with here that I had to get help with my dogs in the kitchen? Am I normal? Did I need help?*

To have the confidence to bring this up in a mock coaching session started a path down liberation, but it still took work to move past the triggers. I had to retrain my brain to continually remind myself that it was okay for them to be gated in the kitchen, because we took excellent care of them. Further, if we worked outside of the home, they would be locked up or possibly even in a cage for a full day. The coaching dramatically helped me past most of the guilt of "Kitchen Gate," pun intended.

It was years later when I was working on an article about playing with Barbies in the basement with my younger sister that my clear mind (thank you meditation!) led me down the path of connecting some dots stemming from childhood. My mother was very strict about where we were allowed to play as children. If we didn't have to use the restroom, we were in the basement or outside if it was nice. She would sit for hours and watch her soap opera or read a romance novel. I used to take a bike ride for hours and had the feeling that she had no clue I was even gone. I also used to sneak away with a friend, taking the bus to the mall. I was in my early teens. Again, gone for hours, and she never knew. Nowadays, with the awareness of sex trafficking, I bet it would be a scary thing for parents. Since I was the oldest child, I was well aware of the feeling of being "locked-in or locked-out" somewhere. I don't think my brother or sister had the same awareness as I did. My need for escape developed early as a child, leading to my strong desire to go away to college and not come back. These memories were playing out in the guilt about my three dogs. It was bringing back locked-in thoughts from childhood that I needed to clear.

My second example is my husband's thought loops. You may know off the top of your head what triggers you about your partner, but do you know what it is about you that triggers them? Ryan's thought loops are a trigger for me.

Your task- find the confidence to ask them. And then have a date night discussion.

We know what Ryan's was about me- my tone. And again, change doesn't happen overnight. It takes work, and unfortunately, tone is something I will always have to work on. Ryan has gotten very good at rephrasing statements in which he figures my tone may come out, so he cuts it off at the door. Not an easy task, but the work has paid off. It's a joint effort of my awareness and his reframing.

Do you know what I mean by loops? There are mind loops that are internal thoughts you keep thinking about over and over in your head. Often stories, and most often negative. Loops can also show up verbally; i.e. you speak them out loud. It's as if you told a story, but then you also repeat it maybe once or more. Normally, a repeated story is one that is bad and also has negative energy. Do you or your spouse do this?

Ryan has loops where he goes on and on about something that isn't necessary to go on and on about. It could be something simple, and there is no energy attached from either of us. But, the "on and on" creates energy. It's like that saying, "If it's not broken don't fix it." Imagine that something you have, like a radio, is working fine. The radio made one little blip, but then you start taking it apart to fix it and find the error only to make it worse, and now you are frustrated, and it is broken. It wasn't broken to begin with, but your fiddling broke it. And now you are pissed off, and your energy is off the positive railroad tracks. There was no real reason to take it apart, but you did.

That's what was happening in our house. A simple statement such as, "I have to cancel tomorrow's charter because of the weather," was initially fine with me. It is what it is when you run a fishing charter business. Weather is the boss. We have always been financially fine with cancelations. We have an abundant mindset, and the clients appreciate the honesty about the weather. When you take a client out in rough weather and they have a terrible time, and maybe even puke their guts out, they don't come back. Many captains don't cancel or reschedule a charter due to weather because they just want to make money. This is a resort practice in which other captains feel, "They will never see them again anyways, so who cares." Burn and turn. Clients that we have canceled on call us the next time that they are in The Keys because they remember how they were treated. My reaction from day one has been, *"No problem, sounds good."* My mindset, *"We are good, and it all works out perfectly for us."*

It didn't happen all at once, but over time we worked through these unnecessary mind loops that lead to falling off the positive railroad tracks. Someday, perhaps, we will be confident enough to laugh when we talk about the weather and it actually brings positive energy...hmm....we will see!

CHAPTER 8

Money

"Face your fears and doubts, and new worlds will open to you." —Robert Kiyosaki

The topic of money can stop you in your tracks, right? Why is that? And where would we be without talking about money in a book about couples and relationships? Before we dive into this chapter, here are the reflection questions:

1. Wealth:
    a. Impossible
   OR
    b. Possible
2. Why do you feel that way?

For some couples it's the elephant in the room. For some couples the male may handle it all and the female knows nothing. That's how I grew up. In our world, I handle it all because Ryan sucks at it. But, what's laughable sometimes is that I am not great at it, either. I don't suck, but I am no financial planner.

Yep, I put it out there. He sucks at it. I remember when we first got together. Now, keep in mind we got married quickly. We dated and lived together for slightly over a year. I knew what he made for a salary, so that was on the table. We split things starting out and he was generous with paying for our dates. But when we got together, got married, and started moving forward I couldn't understand why his phone was ringing all the time.

His phone was ringing non-stop. I couldn't figure out what was going on. Thoughts were always racing through my mind. *Who is calling him? Why is he not answering? Is it a girl? Is he cheating? Is he wanted for something bad? He made a decent salary, better than the statistical average, and then there was my salary. OMG, it's creditors! Why are creditors calling him?*

We finally had to sit down and have a heart to heart. Are you ready for this? This system he created, *pay when they call*, is how he managed his bills....when he remembered. Yep, when he remembered. And then the company would get paid for several months at a time, which would take up his whole paycheck. So for example, he would forget or choose to not pay his car loan, and then when he finally remembered or picked up the phone from the company he would pay for all of the months he had missed. He would pay the late charges, finance fees, and then what was due. His finance management system was a mess, let alone the damage this "financial system" had done to his credit score.

If someone could have come and picked me up off the floor that day, they would have seen I was five shades of white. Have you ever heard of such financial skills? I am no financial planning expert by any means, I have had my share of financial experiences, but this was an "interesting" way to manage money. (My nice way to put things.)

What did we do? It was one of the many "come to Jesus" moments, and was very stressful. But necessary to figure out. I took over. Ends up, Ryan didn't like managing money. He doesn't to this day. Which is a bit concerning to me, but we deal with it. It took me a few months to get caught up on bills, consolidate insurance, our phones, and many expenses which were unnecessary and we were paying too much for separately. It was a good exercise, I guess, and one we laugh about now, but at the time it was stressful, shocking, and overwhelming.

Why don't couples discuss finances? Why is it uncomfortable? We all get a little eye-rolly when we blame it on our parents, but there is truth in that. As Gen X-ers, we were told by our Baby Boomer parents not to talk about money; that it was, "none of my business." I think my mom said none of your business so many times to me that I can still hear her voice in my head. Not talking about money with your children does damage. Truth. Layer on the fact that we don't learn about money in school. I even think about how my grandfather never took time with my mom or me to help us learn. He was sitting on my grandparent's nice allotment of finances that he inherited being married to my grandmother, doing a great job managing it, and never taught us.

Can I change any of this? No, obviously not, and I don't have ill wishes or bad energy towards any of my family, but it's fascinating to learn from, and even more important, crucial to understand why your behavior is such so that you can learn, grow, and move forward.

Circling back to my husband, who is of the same generation as well as his parents, they didn't discuss any financials either, so the pattern is obvious.

After a few months, we had our act together as far as being organized with our finances. However, we were living the Vida Loca in downtown Minneapolis. When I stop to think that we were easily spending $300 or more a weekend on food and drinks, it's a bit much. It could have even been more; those were just the weekends that I felt more aware. We lived downtown and took full advantage of the scene. It would have been nice to be more responsible, when I look back. But, I cannot change that.

A lot of people beat themselves up for the choices they have made financially. This includes debt, about which I shifted my mindset a long time ago to refer to as 'leveraged income'. Shifting your thoughts, words, and feelings around debt can be not only liberating, but life changing, as your feeling affects The Law of Attraction.

Money always flows to me is one of the easiest and most fun affirmations to say. Try it!

In our minds, we started to get ready to "move". The goal was for me to find a job that moved us somewhere south, preferably Florida. The new company would pay for the relocation, a salary, and a signing bonus. When that wasn't working out as planned and we finally made the decision to move, we had nothing. We had our weekly $500 Minnesota unemployment and some money we borrowed (and paid it all back), but that was it. $500 is nice for unemployment, but it doesn't go as far as one would hope. I cut back on all expenses. Everything I could think of got the ax. We switched to peanut butter and jelly sandwiches and happy hour beers only. No fancy dinners, vacations, clothes, or spending that could not be considered building our business towards the future.

Years later, things started to turn. Yes, it took years because Ryan never found a job in which the income came in quickly. It took me two years to understand how to make money in sales in Florida. No one taught me any of this and I wasn't from Florida, so it was a learning process. From that job, every penny extra was poured into our fishing boat and business, The Good Karma.

Now fast forward a few years into Good Karma Sportfishing. Bookings were picking up, which was exciting. I was getting more and more in tune with my intuition and understanding mindset, manifestation, The Law of Attraction, affirmations, positive thinking, gratitude, etc. I had been innately practicing these tools for years without any idea that they were real teachings.

I was so excited to discover a cornucopia of content! Hundreds, maybe even thousands of books written, coaches, courses, and I even discovered Abraham Hicks. Wow! A whole world of modalities that

I could dial in to, practice, and apply even more than I was innately doing. How fun!

I dove in head-first and I took Ryan with me! I immersed him in all of my learnings. But, truth be told, some days he listens, some days he doesn't.

Here's the thing, most couples don't take their partner with them or even try because they may feel that they don't have a partner who is open and willing to learn. How do you change that? You keep chipping away at it. It may not happen overnight, but keep sharing information and don't give up.

Fast forward again a few years and our charter fishing business bookings were up over the previous year, but financially we were just getting by. Every month was the same pattern, and I would end up paying for something with my commission sales job. The charter business wasn't growing financially.

One day, I got quiet and it came to me. My intuition hit me over the head with a ton of bricks.

Holy shit! We have been doing to this to ourselves! We have been joking around, but the universe doesn't know the difference.

A pattern we were saying out loud was putting negative limitations on our business.

Here's the scene....

Ryan would stand at the white freezer in our living room, rigging baits as he got ready for a charter and say, "I am just a poor fisherman."

Close by, I would hear him and chime, "That's okay honey, as long we can pay our bills, we are fine."

This conversation was consistent, at least once a week. He said it as a joke. I would say my rebuttal with all loving intention, as I didn't want him to get discouraged or feel like a failure for not making a lot of money. I joked along.

But, in the eyes of the universe we were creating our money limitations.

That day I woke up. Yes, I woke up.

As he went to say it again, I froze and my eyes opened really wide! I stopped him cold.

"Ryan! we have been causing the limitations and we need to shift what we are saying ASAP!"

I explained my thought process and I knew I was right! That day we stopped the joke. We started positive affirmations towards the business and immediately the next month, seriously, we were in the black. Amazing confirmation about The Law of Attraction.

What are you saying to yourself or each other?

There are many more topics to cover on this subject. This chapter is the tip of the iceberg in our relationship. We have learned that money causes freedom, which leads to ease and happiness but also causes stress and anxiety. We have witnessed that money often tears couples apart.

As most of us know and is most commonly written about, our patterns are caused by limiting beliefs that stem from childhood. You may catch your parents still saying things which trigger the limiting belief. I know we have, and we can recognize it now that we are older and have done the work. However, as most of us know about limiting beliefs, most of us don't do the work necessary to change it and still continue the same patterns.

Getting clear and being open about money is an opportunity for growth in a marriage. Confidence to discuss money and have open communication will set you on the right path. When you both get on the same path regarding money, you can likely conquer anything.

CHAPTER 9

Who The "F" Cares?

"Don't let the behaviors of others destroy your inner peace."—The Dalai Lama

Seriously, who cares? I think this is one of the most freeing sayings you can train your mind to believe.

1. Do you ever say this when you are going over a challenge or a problem?
2. Does your partner ever say this?

Let's break it down.....

Think about the last time one of you vented a challenging situation. Normally, you would go back and forth in the event, creating negative energy (remember my Mama Bear example, this comes up here a lot).

Often, we get wrapped up in other people's judgment, lives, material possessions, children, jobs, you name it. We can sit and dissect and judge all day long. Having written before about judgment regarding my mom and how we used to spend time doing things along these lines; it doesn't create a positive energy force, does it? No.

Instead, you are wasting time, precious time I might add, discussing other people's shit. Why?

Think about that.

Sit with that.

Why not spend more time focusing on your relationship, challenges, goals, wins, and accomplishments, etc. These are the things that can help propel you to the next level.

And by the end of this chapter, I want you to say, *Who Cares?*

Remember in the intro when I mentioned the feedback I used to receive on my annual reviews? "Melinda, just worry about yourself, you are very talented, but you need to learn to work with other people." I came to realize this to be true a few years later, after I had moved on from job to job. It was a useful piece of feedback.

My second job out of college was with Spiegel catalog. Spiegel was a very large catalog retailer which is no longer in business. I interviewed and got a job as a planner, but had to go through their training program first for three months. I was okay with being a trainee until I was placed in a clothing division and sat next to another girl named Adrienne.

Adrienne was hired the same day as me but didn't have to go through the training program. She was placed as a planner on day one. To this day, I have no clue why. As I got to know her, I learned that we both had the same background working in a retail store in management for six months. We also went to similar colleges, earned the same degree, had the same background, were the same age, but yet she didn't have to go through the training program.

Wow, this made my blood boil every time I looked at her. In my competitive eyes, she was three months ahead of me regarding getting promoted to be a buyer. Being a buyer was my goal, and I dreamt of being a buyer since my mother had owned a store when I was a child.

Oh my goodness, as I sit typing this story, I realize just how ridiculous I was. I made up this entire story in my head. I literally made up a story that because she had three months additional planning experience, she would be promoted three months sooner. Seriously, WTF?!

Now it's nothing, but back then three months was a lifetime. And what crystal ball told me she was going to get promoted? None. But there I was, heavy in competition and worrying about the other person.

I was promoted to assistant buyer a week after she was. That week when I was waiting to hear if I had also received a promotion felt like the longest week ever; it was painful. But again, a week! Seriously.

And then, as life would have it, the company started to fold. There were significant problems with shipping orders. They implemented a new warehouse and computer system and they were poorly executed. There wasn't anything to do while we waited, so all of us were working on our resumes during the day. Resumes were flying off the printers like little paper airplanes. Spiegel became a sinking ship and we were jumping overboard; it was a disaster.

The state of Spiegel was a signal for me to move to NYC and land my dream job (or so I thought) at Saks Fifth Avenue. I moved to NYC and left Spiegel and Adrienne behind. About a year later, I learned that she left retail, got married, and had a baby. We ended up randomly speaking on the phone one day while I was living in NYC and she was super cool. I felt like a fool; embarrassed and sad that I wasted so much energy thinking about her. At 22 years old, there was a whole lifetime ahead of me, and I was focused on competing with someone who didn't care about making it to CEO. Can you say wasted energy?

The hindsight of my competitiveness was an enormous learning moment, but I am glad I learned it at that age, as I never felt that way again. There are people ahead of you and you have no idea what their desires are or where their lives will take them. So, to focus any of your precious energy on them is truly a waste.

In the past few years, someone may have been watching me as a top sales rep and been envious. While inside my brain, I had no desire to be a sales rep selling someone else's product and getting a small cut. No one knew that except Ryan; I didn't want to lose my income, so I never told anyone.

Even famous successful actors fall off the screen or take a break. Cameron Diaz and Kate Hudson are great examples of women who quit making movies to take a different path. Years ago, I am sure they had other actresses viewing them as long-term competition.

We often bring competition, worry, or jealousy home with us. People can become consumed with other people. And for what purpose? Again, wasted energy. Say, *who cares?* And focus on yourself.

As a couple, Ryan and I stopped dissecting other people's business many years ago. When he first started Good Karma Sportfishing, I realized he was bringing home thoughts regarding other captains' businesses such as, "So and so got a new boat," and, "So and so is booked every day." "So and so keeps too many undersized fish."

Say it with me, *Who Cares?*

When you break it down and think through those things, you can start to make it a rule to stop the conversation.

I finally had to have the confidence to start saying to Ryan, *Who cares?* All of a sudden one day I thought to say this, and it popped out of my mouth. Ever have those moments? The inside voice becomes your outside voice? And your eyes pop wide open with your own surprise. Like you threw up the words?

Ryan stopped in his tracks and looked at me. My comment, *Who cares?* stunned him silent. The good thing was that innately he understood the message. Ryan didn't get defensive, which is something someone may do. He understood what I was driving towards.

I further added, *Let's think about ourselves. If you need to tell a story, that's fine. But we definitely have enough to work on and talk about.*

We started a practice of breaking this down into three bite-sized bits to diffuse our judgmental thoughts.....

1. Be so busy that you don't have time to care about what the other person is doing.
2. Realize no one is you and you are not them.
3. Do you really want their life? Really?

As an example, I know I don't want their kids, their overhead, or their house. So, I am not jealous.

Done, moving on, *who cares?*

The *Who Cares? Movement* (Yes, I just made it a movement) can be helpful internally, as well. You may not need to speak it out loud if you are managing thoughts or triggers you have. Or, you can share this with your partner and they can manage their own practice managing their thoughts. Straight up, think to yourself, *Who Cares?* And move on. I have found it beneficial to start to practice it internally. Look around you, use social media as an example. There is a lot of content you can easily look at and practice with, let's be honest. Start to look at someone's post and say to yourself, "who cares?" If that person triggers you or has bad energy, this can diffuse it quickly. It takes the energy right out and releases it.

But often, as a good partner you need to listen. We have practiced shifting to saying first, "I need to vent." Get it off your chest. If you can do this, talk about venting as I mention in Chapter 10, be upfront with expectations, and then roll on; that's cool. It may help you mentally if you are good at or get good at releasing the story. Remember, it's a story. However, the caveat is to not keep going on and on about it. Say it and move off the topic.

I debated also adding in what some other coaches recommend as a tip, and that is, "sitting in it." But I don't believe sitting in it does anyone any good. Hence why authentically, I cannot add that as one of my tips. Sitting in the venting, judging, and discomfort only extends the energy. And before you know it, both of you have the same negative energy. Therefore, both of you are off the positive railroad tracks.

Let's get on the same railroad tracks...

You can take this to the same level with your children, too. Your daughter came home upset because Jodi next door has new designer jeans. This is definitely easier said than done. However, if you get her to realize her power and ability to diffuse the energy, she will get stronger and learn to focus on herself.

What's the very popular quote?

"Where attention goes energy flows!"

I am sure you have heard that saying before. Many people have requoted the saying, tweaked it a bit, and attached their name.

Do you know what it means? Have you ever really sat with that and thought about the meaning and how that affects what you are trying to achieve from a universal standpoint? If you sit around focusing on someone else, which, by the way, has nothing to do with you, doesn't affect you, and you can't change it, the energy flows to that person. In addition, if you focus on competition, The Law of Attraction will bring more competition to you.

I am mentioning energy a lot in this chapter, but it's important.

The energy, focus, and feeling all go hand in hand. And the feeling is what you want to get good at to manifest your dreams.

Another good saying that is as old as the hills is, "Worry about yourself." I grew up with my mom saying it to me, time and time again.

But no one ever explained what it meant when you dug in. I'm not even sure if she understood or not herself, but it doesn't matter. Focus on yourself, focus your energy on yourself, and watch your desires grow.

> "Worrying is using your imagination to create what you don't want."- Abraham Hicks

We all know those worriers in our lives. Let's all change worrier to warrior!

CHAPTER 10

Are You Both In it to Win it?

Values and What If Only One is in the Game?

*H**eck yeah! I'm in it to win it- what about you?*

"It's not hard to make decisions when you know what your values are."—Walt Disney

If I asked you to sit down and write out your three core values and then also your partner's three core values,

1. What would they be?
2. Would they match or mirror?

You may not remember this, but there used to be a TV show called *Love Connection*. The show ran for 11 years, from 1983-1994, and Chuck Woolery was the host. I was addicted. Andy Cohen brought it back as the host is 2017, but unfortunately, it was canceled. But, it was good while it lasted! Ryan and I watched the episodes with Andy Cohen together. He also remembered watching the original ones with Chuck Woolery.

Many love connections were made on the show, and it was fun to see their answers and cheer the love matching on. It provoked a sense of curiosity and hope. In addition, what I took from the show was a lesson in values. Most often, the couple was a match because the answers they gave stemmed from their core belief system; something a lot of us take for granted or don't recognize.

Have you heard this before?

"I have a dream and my partner isn't supportive."

I have heard partners say it before many times. Go into any business private Facebook group and you will see posts and/or comments from a partner regarding lack of support. It's a reality and it can suck. Often, a partner may stifle the other person.

A lot of that has to do with values, as well as values in conjunction with not knowing or understanding. The lack of knowing or understanding leads down a path of gathering confidence regarding communication.

How do you start to unravel this and get on the same page?

Values define us. Values coincide or clash with what another person thinks or acts upon.

If you think about it, how you feel about your values and how perceptive you are to your own, let alone others', can lead to success or failure.

How does this come into play with confidence? Good question! When you understand your values, you can use or build the confidence to control what you need to control.

On the flipside, recognizing other people's values lets you release that control and move forward. Remember- you can only control yourself. Not the other person. The Serenity Prayer is a great tool to help. Even if you are not religious or spiritual, it can still be a helpful tool. You can take it as face value for an affirmation that can help get your mindset in the right place.

Serenity Prayer:

> God, grant me the serenity to accept the things I cannot change, courage to change the things I can, and wisdom to know the difference. - Reinhold Niebuhr

I remember in the corporate world we would painstakingly review the company core values and then forget about them. They were never implemented or even recognized after the annual meeting. No one ingrained them into the culture. They were words on a piece of paper or on a white board which was revisited every year when you planned your sales goals for the upcoming fiscal year. Have you had the same experience? Unfortunately, a lot of people relate to values for the same reason, hence the resonance isn't there like it should be.

Now sit and think about your values. Here is a data dump list in case you are stuck:

Timeliness
Cleanliness
Loyalty
Honesty
Family
Health/Fitness
Money
Safety
Positivity
Charity
Hard work
Vacation/relax

Gratitude/Appreciation
Professionalism

Values can instilled, changed, positive, negative, as well as determined by behavior and conditioning.

After you think about your values, what can you do to start the conversation with your partner?

This is another communication starter. You both can take the list above and rank them. Compare notes and discuss. Truly listen to each other so you can learn.

When I think about all of the stories I have shared so far in this book, we can trace every outcome to values. When you value each other, you spend time working on the challenges you may have. You find time to communicate. You discuss triggers and help each other work through them. You understand that energy affects everything and it's important to stay positive. Money values are discussed and worked through. Values are all-encompassing keys to success in every level of your life. Start today by recognizing yours. It's a whole new day. No wait....

It's a whole new world!!! —Cue *Alladin* music
As Ryan would say, "Please help me!"

CHAPTER 11

I Need Space - Setting Boundaries

"Sometimes there is more magic in "I miss you" than "I love you." —Anon

Over the years, I have noticed a lot of power in giving each other space and setting boundaries. I feel these can go hand in hand. Having the strength and communication skills to do so is a big part of getting this puzzle piece to fit correctly.

First, let's attack the space part, because this often comes up and it can be the elephant in the room that many couples do not address.

Reflection questions:

1. What do you think of when your partner says, "I am going on a boys (or girls) weekend."?

2. How do you make use of your time when the other person is away?
3. How often are you checking your phone/emails/texts?

Over the years, I am always surprised at how many couples I meet who have challenges with being separated for periods of time. I don't mean in some lovey-dovey way, but more of a control situation.

When you lack confidence in being apart from each other, i.e. trust or comfort in yourself, it can wreak havoc on a relationship.

There are many ways to dissect this prevalent issue.

A. Can't be alone
B. Jealousy
   OR!
C. You are downright worried something happened

Let's have fun covering all three....

I believe I manifested my husband, Ryan. I asked the universe for a husband who was tall with dark curly hair, a big smile, and a hobby. Be careful what you wish for. He matched the physical description and bonus! He even had the hobby....fishing. Granted, fishing is now his business, but at the time we met, it was his hobby. He spent long hours at the river, dam, Lake Michigan, smaller local lakes, basically anywhere he could throw a line on a fishing pole in the water. Like I skipped school as a teenager to go to the mall, he skipped work as an adult to go fishing.

When we first started Good Karma Sportfishing, there were many times I used to think, *Is he ever coming home? Do I need to call for help?*

I don't consider myself a worry wort, but I am only human, and this pushed the boundaries of communication. Have you ever been there?

Ryan is one of those determined people. People ask me if I go fishing a lot; actually, they assume I do, and honestly, I don't. Why? Because there is always "one more spot to try," *and I have to pee!*

So, what happens? He is "being Ryan" and forgets to let me know he is staying out late. Not hearing from him can be maddening. Imagine- your husband is on a boat in the ocean, often we have crazy storms that pop up, and he is late. My human brain can easily take over and lead me down a dark path of worry. And I don't enjoy worrying! It does not feel good, and it's always my intention to feel good.

We recently had a similar situation in which I thought he was already back at the dock in his car heading home. We live less than 10 minutes from the marina. When it got to be over a half hour later, I started to think to myself, *Am I worried, or is he okay?* I used my intuition to guide me, and it led me to know he was okay. He indeed was fine. The text he sent me was confusing, and it turned out that he wasn't back at the dock yet, after all, he was on his way back. Two different things and a time difference of about an hour. *Whew!*

It's taken awhile, but we have had some training. Yes, I said it, "training."

I don't enjoy having a minor heart attack, face breakouts, or hair loss wondering where the heck he is. I'll openly admit that it has taken years of training to push through this and some other things. Call it what you will, but we all have those little things that add up and also are triggers. One of mine, putting the remote control in the holder on the coffee table...I digress.

In addition to worry, many partners are often afraid to be alone. I can understand the fear from the standpoint that I didn't meet Ryan and get married until I was almost 35. Looking back, 35 isn't old at all, but we all know most people do have marriage ticker (and some also have a baby clock) going off in their brains. I was one of those people. The excitement to finally "meet the man of my dreams" also caused anxiety regarding "what if I lose him?". The fear of loss coincides with the lack of confidence that nothing will ever tear you apart. Some partners get over the fear in time; some don't and may have deeper challenges to overcome.

The good part is that you can overcome your fears when you start to recognize the origin. This is extremely important to remember for all challenges, fears, anxiety, depression, etc. Take time to identify the origin so you can communicate with each other and move forward.

The "origin." "Eek! The word itself feels heavy, let alone the unpacking. I don't know about this...."

Learning and understanding the origin of your fear is a significant process. Don't get caught up in the time needed or judge yourself about the source once you realize. It could be something that brings shame, embarrassment, anger, resentment, etc.; a mix of emotions which many people don't want to ever discuss. Let things unfold as they should and have compassion- for yourself, your partner, and others involved.

As I mentioned, the origin of my fear was from being single for so long. If I had a nickel for every time someone said to me, "Why don't you have a boyfriend?" I would be rich. The thought of that question still makes my blood curdle. My heart goes out to every single person who has to deal with that question, too. When I was a merchant for Victoria's Secret, I desperately wanted a boyfriend. I talked about finding a boyfriend all the time. I was obsessed.

One day, My VP's admin told me I should visit her church and I would surely meet my dream man. She was overly passionate and convincing. She had met her husband at this church, so I saw a flicker of hope for me. Her church held service on Sunday evenings and the church was a far drive from my apartment in Columbus, Ohio. It was on the other side of town and over an hour's drive into the country. I didn't know where I was going, and back then, GPS, cell phones, etc., did not exist. I kept driving and driving through the dark and the snow. The trek was a bit nutty, but the hope that

I would meet the man of my dreams at this church and God would answer my prayers kept me going.

I arrived at what she referred to as a church. I did a double-take and chose to refer to it as a stadium. The place was enormous! They had a live band, not just a piano and a harp, but a full band. TV cameras were everywhere, and the place was jamming! There were so many people; I was overwhelmed and out of my mind, confused about where I was. I had grown up attending a small, white wood Presbyterian church in the hills. I had never seen, nor attended, a church like this church. The pastor even did a segment speaking in tongues!

This huge ass church with lights and glitter (kidding on the glitter) was something else. As the service went on, there was a segment where you turned to your neighbors in the pews and asked them what they were asking from God. A "speak it out loud" moment. The neighborly requests went on for at least 15 minutes. My ask was, *To find a boyfriend and fall in love.* Everyone else, I kid you not, was, "To get out of debt." I didn't return as my intuition told me it wasn't a good fit. I felt boyfriend material was a bit unlikely. Oh well! Noting ventured, nothing gained, right?

Another huge challenge that can frequently pop up for many couples is the ugly green monster, aka **jealousy.**

I have to admit; my main competition is fish. My husband's wedding vows stated, "I don't know if I can ever love anything more than fishing." Truth. *What the heck?*

But, even with the oddity that statement is, we have made it work. A testament that you can always make it work. I knew up front the mindset I was dealing with, right? I FINALLY met someone;, a tall, cute boy with a big smile and a hobby. I had done the work on myself regarding my expectations of what the perfect partner is. I was okay with letting go and understanding compromise. In conjunction, I am an independent woman, so I didn't need my partner to be with me 24/7. I have learned through the years that I like being alone. Many partners do need, or feel they need, to be with someone all the time. Why? What thought pattern or belief is driving that? Ryan's desire to go fishing, or even take a nap, was a break for me to have my alone time. Recognizing what you need and then how it relates is an essential step in the relationship journey.

Open communication regarding you and your partner's desires and intentions takes any misunderstanding or elephants out of the room. It's on the table. It is then your choice to deal with it, compromise, accept, or walk away. Remember, there is always a choice.

All of these examples circle back to communication, and also laying down boundaries.

In the simplest definition, found on Google, personal boundaries:

"Help you define what you are comfortable with, and how you would like to be treated by others."

Boundaries are my favorite topic and are life-changing. That's a fact. Once you get the confidence to have open discussions and communication, boundaries are a natural evolution.

Ask yourself, what you are willing to accept? What's a "no"? What's more grey?

When I work with people on boundaries, I have found a few things about boundaries to be true for most people:

- They are people pleasers.
- They hope for the best but know it may not work out.
- They lack the confidence to say no.

It's amazing how often, eventually, the lack of boundaries leads to disappointment and frustration.

How do you see yourself? Are you aware? How have you worked to overcome? Have you communicated your challenge to your partner? And vice versa?

There is a great quote I have heard many times,

> "The only people that get upset about you setting boundaries are the people that benefit from you having none."—Unknown.

Take a second to think about that quote. It's true, isn't it? If someone is your friend or meant to be in your life, you can have a positive energy-neutral conversation in which you set or exchange boundaries. It's very healthy if it's a conversation and the other person's point of view is also considered.

Asking Ryan to do a better job communicating about his ETA after a charter is a boundary. It's a boundary for my health- mentally and physically. It took time to get to a better place, as his limiting belief was that someone (not necessarily me) was trying to control him. Ryan's belief stemmed from his childhood, as he often stayed out late fishing and his parents would have to come to look for him with flashlights. We communicated and pushed past that belief to arrive at an understanding that helps both parties.

There are always solutions. Believe it or not, things always work out. And they work out for the Greater Good. I hadn't fully grasped the message with that saying until 2020. It coincides with, "What's meant to be is meant to be," which I heard a lot growing up. If you can release the challenge, give it a rest, some thought, prayers, and take out the energy, a solution will appear that is in the best interest of all parties, and things will be okay. Try it...no...better yet...Do it!

CHAPTER 12

Do What Feels Good

As we work on our relationship (yes, newsflash, relationships are work and it never ends...) I keep circling back to a statement I say to Ryan: "Do what feels good."

What does this mean? It means, make the decision that leads you down the path to feel good.

It sounds simple, but how do you build the confidence to do that?

And why is that such a difficult concept to understand?

Society has norms and expectations. People do, as well. We often live and operate within a construct of doing what people expect without often realizing everything is a choice.

You decided to get up today. You didn't have to. You truly have the option to stay in bed. You are likely saying to yourself, "Well Melinda, I have kids to take care of, how do you suppose I stay in bed?" or "I have a job to get to."

But, if you sit and think about it long and hard, everything is a choice. Albeit, it's not a great option to ignore your children or skip work, I get it, but it is a choice. As I walk you through this next scenario, think back to examples in the past or recent examples and break them down. You will start to realize it.

I learned two things my Freshman year at Purdue University. And yes, my parents know about this so don't worry. One was my social security number. Back then (in the olden days before computers), our grades were taped to the hallway walls and listed by social security number. We obviously weren't worried about cyber security, either.

And the second thing I learned in college was that everything is a choice.

I had an accounting 101 teacher who told us on our first day of class, "Everything is a choice, you can decide not to come to class, not to do your homework, or not to take an exam. You have a choice."

I sat in disbelief...wondering.... *What the hell was he talking about? My dad paid for my education and expects me to graduate on time. I have to attend class! Is he nuts?* I sat with it and let the message sink in. I have never forgotten it.

As I sat there pondering his statement with my mind spinning, I remembered when I was a kid and my mom would make stew, which I hated with a passion. She would say to me, "If you don't eat your dinner you have to sit in the corner." I made the confident choice to sit in the corner. I hated the stew that much, and honestly, I liked sitting in the corner. *Hum...Is that odd?* ......I digress.

I ask you to do the same; sit with my accounting teacher's statement and your memories of choices and let it sink in. Now, you don't want to take it to the extreme like I did and skip the exam to go get a fake ID and drink up some cocktails at Harry's (the popular bar on campus). Not the best example, but again it was a choice. I ended up repeating the class my senior year, stressed out, biting my nails, worried I wouldn't graduate on time. Real life choice in action! And choices often have consequences if they are not for the highest good.

If you follow any manifestation coach or spiritual teacher/guide such as Abraham Hicks, the feeling part, i.e. "feeling good", is a huge component. I strongly suggest that you take this concept and apply it. Not just at the level of meditation, but making it a solid decision-making factor in how you move through your choices.

When you start to remember and think about it, it makes sense. We are all responsible for ourselves. Your wellbeing and happiness is something YOU control. For example, as I write this chapter there is an extreme amount of election result chaos in the world. But I cannot control that. I can, however, control my desire to feel good, hence I am ignoring it. I have made the decision to ignore it. If it does come across my path, I make the decision to not let it affect me. I am reminding myself that I cannot control it at this point in time. People voted, it's done, moving on.

Be so busy being happy and doing what you love that you can easily tune out the noise.

We live by this, and being that we are both very busy, it has proven itself to be true. But yes, some days we need a reminder to get back on track.

Ryan has a very active, private, free Facebook community. He does his best to manage the content so it is positive, collaborative, and continues on the path building a great community. The other day he approved someone, but shortly after realized that the person's intention for joining may not be for the highest good. He immediately thought to kick him out. My Mama Bear stepped in and was like, "Sure, kick him out, whatever you want to do, I have your back." We both calmed down a bit and regrouped. Ryan and I both took a few deep breaths.

Ryan reflected on the situation, "Does this cause me any harm? And how do I feel about it?"

He took time to think about how he felt, and he didn't feel good thinking he should kick him out. Needless to say, he left him in the group, which ended up being a positive decision.

It's okay to take a step back, breathe, even take a nice long pause and think about how your actions make you feel. Often, we cannot take them back. Isn't it better to take some time to think about it first vs. living with regret?

This thought process easily jibes with social media posting and the keyboard warrior syndrome. Before you react to something, take a moment, think, breath, and either walk away or make a choice to respond.

There is a vast difference between reacting and responding. Reacting is the keyboard warrior. I would confidently say we have all been there at least once. You get so fired up and type an email or post and hit send and then you say to yourself, "Oh shit, did I really do that?" And then you have a mess to clean up.

When I started as a sales rep, I worked with a manufacturer. The owner was a hothead, to say the least. One second, he was the nicest, kindest big brother-like person in the world who you would give your right arm to, and then five seconds later he could rip your head off. No joke. It was scary at times, and there were countless occasions where he brought me to tears. The shock value was enough to make my blood curl and give me nightmares.

I remember when I was first starting the position, we were trying to get an order going with a large retailer. There were so many emails flying around, I was dizzy. He ended up firing off a heated email to me regarding the buyer. Oh, it was bad....really bad. The worst name calling and screaming over email I have ever seen, if you can imagine. He ended up sending the nasty email to the buyer, too, by mistake.

Can you say, "SHIT!!!!!!!" really loud? I was a new rep and it was an account I was going to be taking over. I saw the dollar signs float right past my head. I almost passed out cold on the floor from shock. He called me frantically about the email he had mistakenly sent to her which was meant for me. The crazy thing is, he was so brilliant, he came up with a solution to bombard her with so many emails from both of us. The goal was to bury the nasty email as she would be deleting them and reading only the latest.

Hope you are sitting for this....it worked. The buyer never said a word, it must have been deleted.

The moral of the story is: Save yourself the panic and drama and don't react.

Make a conscious choice to respond vs. react- Process and walk away before you speak or send. Do you think I will ever forget this story? Likely not.

One thing that has stuck out to me as a coach since I started in this space is the judgment and opinion concerning walking away from people or situations. I find that it is often advised, "You are the issue and you are the one that needs to do the work," almost like a forced direction to change based on someone else's point of view, and doubtfully based on the full story.

Why do coaches or therapists often put the ownership on the person? This "it's your fault - own it" mindset can make someone feel bad about themselves, which doesn't feel good. And even if you do the work, the other person likely isn't doing the work and you will keep butting up against the same icky feeling.

Of course, there is ALWAYS work to be done. Have you ever heard the phrase, "It takes two to tango?" I have always resonated with that saying. I first do a deep dive on the situation to see if it is me. I sit with something, ponder it, and try my hardest not to feel icky. Maybe try a few solution-oriented actions in case it is me, do the work on my end ...but then I have to decide. Again, you can make a choice.

I'll share this example:

I met a fellow healer a few years back at an event. I was excited to meet someone in the space who I could collaborate with, we didn't compete as I am a coach and speaker and she is a therapist with a yoga studio. It was a win-win, and I was excited about this relationship as we were both looking to build our businesses. However, after nine months, I had to walk away. It started to dawn on me that the relationship was one-sided. I was spending my time, energy, and knowledge to always help her and nothing ever came in return. I had promoted her on my podcast, referred people to her studio for her events, spent time coaching her with valuable info that most coaches charge for, and supported her on social media platforms. Since my nature is to be a giver, it did take some time to finally wake up. Ryan started to warn me about three months prior that she just wasn't on the same page, and he was confused as to why I was still helping her. He believed that I needed to be focusing on my business, and there are only so many hours in a day. Why was I spending any more time helping her when nothing was being reciprocated? I greatly appreciated his support from someone watching the situation from outside, and he had met the other person. But, I was still supporting her and it was becoming an energy drain conflicted with guilt.

The final straw was when I was hosting my monthly meetup, and at the last minute she decided not to attend. The reason was fascinating, and I can see both sides. Boundaries on her end, but I also had to wake up to the fact that it wasn't anything life threatening and she was choosing to let something control her vs. choosing to support someone, a friend.

It was an interesting dynamic of boundaries and choices. I still honored my commitment and attended her event the next night. When I counted the people in the room in attendance, and I saw that a quarter of the room attendees were the result of my referral. I knew it was time to move on. I had done my part as a good collaborator, but it was time to ask the universe for new connections who collaborated back. Why? Because, quite frankly, I deserve that. Confidence. I had to confidently walk away.

We are all human, and partnerships, relationships, however you wish to classify, are best when they are two-sided. The energy spent agonizing over the decision and questioning whether I am a good person or not wasn't fair to me. This is also where people who consider themselves 'people pleasers' often struggle. If that's you, you may be afraid to let someone down or think that you are bad for walking away. We are all perfect in the eyes of the universe, so why do we allow others to judge us if we decide to walk away because the relationship doesn't feel good?

Negative energy takes you off your positive train tracks. The other person isn't going to change, nor is it fair for you to have expectations that they change. You cannot control them. **Again, you cannot control them.** But, you can control yourself; your actions, your thoughts. You can bless them and move on. And when you do bless them and move on, you will be amazed at how much better you feel. A huge weight will come off your shoulders.

I read someone's blog the other day which said, "The other person had darkness in them because they walked away from their friendship." In her blog, she said, "The other person had things to work on." Again, two to tango.

Understanding your friends and relationships is the same as understanding your partnership. Why would you want to be in a bad marriage? Bad friendships are the same thought process. If you have done a deep dive on things you question and recognize where the issue comes from, but realize the other person isn't going to change and wonder who you are to even ask them to, then walk away.

On a partnership note, how cool is it that Ryan acknowledged my efforts, encouraged me to make a decision in which I would feel better, and then supported the decision? It's important for me to call this out so you will have those open discussions, as well, if you don't already. When you have someone in your corner who can give an objective opinion, it means the world.

When you feel good, your partner will also feel good.

I have to say, it felt great to walk away! It freed up time and mental space. People talk about organizing their desk or their closet, but organizing your mental space is just as important, if not more important. De-clutter your mind of useless thoughts, worries, and expectations and you will be amazed at how you can focus on what's important in building your confidence and your future.

CHAPTER 13

Teamwork, Support, and the Recipe

First let's chat about teamwork.

"Teamwork is the ability to work together toward a common vision. The ability to direct individual accomplishments toward organizational objectives. It is the fuel that allows common people to attain uncommon results." —Andrew Carnegie

Teamwork is a big part of our marriage. Remember what I told you my dad said for our wedding toast? It's become our reality. To be honest, we do make a very good team. Not always perfect, but no team is, right? You have to delegate, figure out strengths and weaknesses, communicate, take ownership, fix problems, and the list goes on. As you get to know your team and figure things out, your confidence will build.

Reflection questions:

1. Do you see yourself and your partner as a team?
2. In what ways do you operate as a team?
3. What can you improve?

> "It's amazing that you help your husband clean the boat, my wife would never do that." —Good Karma Sportfishing clients.

If I had a nickel for every time I have heard this, I would be uber wealthy. And you may have heard that story before, but it bears repeating because it is something that keeps coming up. No, not my boat cleaning skills, but the fact that it's a surprise to people that we help each other so often. Quite frankly, it's shocking to me that most people don't help each other. I help him unload the car when he gets home, and he helps me unload my car when I have been away.

One story that shocks most people is when I used to be the mate on The Good Karma. Yep, me the fishing mate. Not my skill set at all. However, I have always been someone who can put "racehorse blinders on" and get through it. Frankly, we didn't have a choice. Ryan started Good Karma Sportfishing January, 2012. It is common for all boats to have one or two mates. Good Karma is a 23' boat, so having an extra person can be a bit tight, but at the time we definitely had all intentions of having a mate work with Ryan. We figured it would be challenging finding someone with a solid work ethic who was professional, trustworthy, and showed up, since that isn't the easiest thing to do, especially in The Keys. In addition, the fishing paycheck isn't going to make you a millionaire. Hence, we blew through five mates in less than five months. It was painful. The mate situation dealt with everything from arrogance, to someone landing in jail, to domestic issues. It was a fun time- not. I finally looked at Ryan and said, "I will be the mate and we will save every penny so we can automate this boat and you won't need a mate."

The queen has spoken (LOL!.) Let it be written, let it be done. And it was. We haven't dealt with a mate since that day and have no plans to.

But, it wasn't always that way for everything. I used to have anxiety when returning home from a sales trip because I knew the house would be chaotic. Our three Shih Tzu's would need to go out for potties and there was probably a doggy mess somewhere, things out of place, garbage needing to go out, etc. It's not that Ryan is a bad person or unclean; he is just a bit spacey and tends to be consumed with fishing. *What the heck is going on here? What is that smell? Have the dogs even been looked at today at all?*

So, I realized I needed to give him a heads up when I was on my way home so he could start to get ready before the tornado, which I can become, walked in the door.

You know what? It worked! Step by step, asking for small tasks to be taken care of and then saying "thank you" and other kind words changed the dynamics of our household. Topside it seems manipulative, doesn't it? But then drill it down; isn't this how we should always work towards improving? Kindly asking and then saying thank you. Who cares if there is an agenda? I hate to break it to you, but life is full of agendas and if these small steps towards order in your household work, then do them. *I'd survive being a little manipulative in order to have a clean house. Wouldn't you? Get on the train!*

Do you ever have those irritating nails-on-the-chalkboard moments that may drive you over the edge? Make it a focus to nip those in the bud.

We had a recurring chalkboard situation that was like Groundhog Day in a bad dream. It was painful, and now I often say, "Takeout saved our marriage." Takeout saved our marriage could probably be its own book.

Here is how our loop was happening....

I would travel for sales and be gone for days at a time. Fighting the traffic on my way home, especially through Miami, which is often loaded with rough and aggressive drivers. Miami drivers are ruthless; they are fearless and don't pay any attention to other vehicles. When I would finally pull up after the trip, I would be tired but happy to be home. Imagine being greeted with, "What are we having for dinner?" I would hear tires screeching in my head as Ryan would ask me the question. *WHAT??!!!??? You have got to be kidding! I had just driven over three hours home fighting traffic, unloaded my car, answered urgent "house is on fire" sales calls and emails, got my orders in so they could ship out ASAP, AND FINALLY PEED!!! And you wanted me to cook you dinner, too? What the F have you been doing? Breathe, breathe, breathe. Unload your car and just take a moment.*

Ryan, my sweetheart (sarcasm), truly expected me to get home and cook dinner. Half the time, he was home all day. How was this happening to me? Making dinner and then doing dishes was something I had come to dread.

Until.....Exit 2 appeared like a sun shining after a lot of rainy days. Exit 2 offered a plethora of food options. It was a miracle sent from the heavens. All of the sudden, we had a Chili's, Buffalo Wild Wings, Longhorn, Chipotle, Panera, and even more. Who can I hug and kiss for this amazing city planning? I had hope. Hope I wouldn't kill my husband after my next trip home. And bonus! Gift cards from my family for the holidays became the best gift ever!

Being able to stop at Exit 2 before getting on the final stretch to The Keys goes down as one of the best days of my life. And that's not even considering that I actually like the food! These restaurants are not in The Keys, so it also offered us a well needed change of dining options. The relief of not having to make dinner when I got home from a trip took years off my body and face. So, if you ever think I look young, it's take out. Just kidding, but not really. My dinner team became a bunch of restaurants. My clean and orderly house transpired from confidence to work with Ryan to achieve it.

When Ryan read this chapter, it was a trigger for him. I had no idea that cooking dinner, in his mind, went hand in hand with drinking. In Chapter 2 on Change, I write about the change in drinking. It made me think and believe. If you think about photos of men grilling, they often have a beer in their hand. Perfect Father's Day card!

People cooking dinner may also be drinking a glass of wine as they cook. Have you ever read this meme?

"I cook with wine. Sometimes I even add it to the food."

Or

"I tried cooking with wine last night. After five glasses I forgot why I was in the kitchen."

I have seen these memes time and time again in gift stores on funny cocktail napkins, tea towels, and coasters. It must have some validity, otherwise it wouldn't be on products for sale, right?

I learned two things. First, he was fearful of feeling tempted to start drinking while cooking, as his past behavior and social witnessing drew that pattern in his brain.

Second, he felt I was fussy about food. At first, I didn't quite understand that one, but okay, maybe I am fussy? *Hmm, yeah, last night I thought there was too much tomato sauce on my shrimp and grits, and not enough cheese sauce on the appetizer. Okay, I will own my fussiness.*

Both of these things in combination led to his questioning, "What are you making for dinner?" as a solution for him to deal with his triggers, which was a trigger for me.

Triggers! So many of them, in so many ways. Kind of like all the lottery ticket combinations which can occur. However, I would rather win the lottery than be triggered. I'm sure you would agree.

What do you deal with that is similar? What makes your blood curdle when you are asked? Or do you think to yourself, "If I could just get some help with XYZ then life would be so much better." As I work with clients, I am amazed at the amount of people that do not speak up about these things. They don't even give the other person a chance. I have heard it all from:

"Oh no, he won't do it, so why bother asking?"

"She doesn't do it the way I would like it, so I just do it myself."

At the end of the day the choice is yours. You can continue to have daily/weekly/monthly occurrences where you could have used some help but didn't ask and it bothers you. Or you can have the discussion and work towards a more teamwork-based approach. I vote for giving the other person a chance, taking the time to work through it, and asking for a miracle to finish it up!

Support

The other aspect of teamwork is support. If you feel alone in your partner not supporting your business ideas, or a friendship, or how you raise your children, you are not alone. I am sure you can add to that list, as well.

"My husband doesn't support my new business idea."

"She won't let me buy that extra piece of equipment we need to grow."

"He's so nasty when I come home after hanging out with Cynthia."

Support shows up in all different ways. It also often takes time, so don't give up! Your idea may be new and completely blindside the other person. They may have limiting beliefs that stem from their experience or childhood. Getting to the bottom of "why" they are feeling this way and working on it gently over time will change the thought process.

We have had our fair share of business ideas. Some worked, some didn't. I always say the mistakes build confidence just as much as the wins. Mistakes are lessons.

Ryan desperately wanted a second boat so he could fish the back-country in The Keys when it was too windy on the ocean. We spent close to $100K on a gorgeous brand new boat (including the out-fitting), and that plan didn't work. We learned that Ryan's customer base was not interested in fishing the backcountry. Ryan had built his business on fishing the blue water ocean. The two different bodies of water have different species and are also a different experience. Ryan further realized he wasn't passionate about fishing in the backcountry. Hence, two years later, we sold the boat, paid it off, and moved on.

I swear I was brainwashed at a very popular speaker's event in 2018 in West Palm Beach. I purchased a House Flipping AND an Option Trading course. I think I have blocked that amount out of my brain, as it brings up bad energy and takes me off my positive railroad tracks. I remember coming home, excited, somehow thinking that I was going to be flipping houses like the guy on HGTV and also making millions in trading options. A great NLP salesperson will do that to you.

What was I thinking? What happened to my brain? Can I get out this?

Ends up, after a few days, you can't get out of it. I attended the Options Trading courses and gave it my best shot. It was fascinating because after the second tier of classes, you realize they actually cannot fully train you on how to trade options. It was all mindset training.

Lovely. What a f-ing waste of money and time. I learned a lot that day about events, popular (dare I even say famous) motivational speakers and how they make money, but most of all, I learned that my husband was supportive of me and I of him. You need to try things in life and business. Sometimes they work out and sometimes they don't, but you will push through it and be able to move forward if you communicate and treat each other as a team.

All along, though, we were supportive of each other, and I am grateful. At the end of the day, money is energy, and if your mindset is in the right place, and you bet on yourself, it will bounce back.

I have the confidence that it will- tenfold.

Teamwork and Support in Combination

During the holidays, as I was in the midst of writing this book, my mind was flooded with eye-opening revelations, aka AHA moments. I had received the Ace of Swords tarot card on many occasions. I received this message when pulling cards for myself, as well as during the YouTube readings I watch (more on those in my second book coming out this summer.)

What does the Ace of Swords tell us?

(Taken directly from the tarot card deck- Eight Coins- Tarot Truth by Lana Zellner, Published by U.S. Games Systems, Inc.)

The Ace of Swords comes as a burst of fresh air. It often appears suddenly and unexpectedly, but usually when we are needing it most. The ace is swift and invigorating, a gust of wind sweeping us away from a period of stagnation and back into action.

The man in the card closes his eyes, opens his mind, and lets his ideas lead his path. His sword cuts through the clouds below and holds his crown above his head. The sun comes through the air behind him and signifies the bright new ideas that have finally come to light his path.

Allow the universe to send you a signal and open your mind to the answers you have been looking for. You can't rush the Ace of Swords and you can't force it into your situation. It will come when it's time so keep your eyes open for the opportunity. The new ideas you need will come in like a gust of wind, unexpectedly and quietly. If you keep your senses heightened however, you will not miss it.

I was fascinated as this beautiful card appeared time and time again. I would look up and laugh, *Okay, I get it.*

The sword was cutting through my mind and clarity was flooding me in huge waves.

The AHA moment I had in relation to this chapter, was that I wasn't "owning" my part in the success of Good Karma Sportfishing.

How does this play out? Often, in coaching spaces or with courses and programs, the desired verbiage is, "I am a six-figure entrepreneur." You may even have to fill out a form to be accepted into a mastermind that only includes six-figure entrepreneurs.

I need to confidently state that I am one of them.

In addition to having positive, forward-thinking affirmations which allow The Law of Attraction to manifest, Good Karma Sportfishing is a six-figure business and growing. I was thinking of Good Karma Sportfishing regarding Ryan, but for some reason not including myself. *His business, his success.* Without being a martyr, with all my heart and soul, I celebrated his success. But I was forgetting that I have been the Wizard of Oz, the person behind the curtain, and we have been a team.

My loop went on further as other coaches and programs were triggering me to feel small and like a follower. We successfully created a business even more tangible than others who are only online. We deal with weather, extreme competition, mechanical issues, and client expectations to achieve something that is not always in our control – catching fish. Oh! And don't forget a devastating hurricane in 2017 named Irma. No one in the coaching online space has this experience.

My lack of online presence all these years resulted in me feeling small. Social media has its place, good and bad. I didn't put myself online until 2019, which was very behind the majority of the world and people in the coaching space. That was my choice. I don't live in regret and I can't change my late start; the time machine hasn't been built yet, but it was the result which ended up compounding into the perception of myself.

Again, I need to confidently state, I am one of them.

Ryan has been above and beyond amazing. Many times, he has said to me, "You are my business partner." He gives me credit all the time in his podcast, posts, his Facebook groups, with his clients, and in his newsletter. However, he could feel that I wasn't owning it. He has called me out before. But, as I said in the beginning, the work starts with yourself and I needed to own it. This was my issue to own and change.

When I came back from my walk the morning of the revelation and told Ryan, I could sense he was relieved. I forgot to put this section in the book and when he read it, he reminded me to add it in.

"You need to add in a section about not owning your part in Good Karma Sportfishing," Ryan suggested.

Yep, I do.

Ryan is an incredible partner, and I am confidently owning our success! We all have things to own in our life. My story is meant to inspire you to take a look and see what you can own.

> "You've always had the power my dear, you just had
> to learn it for yourself." – Glinda The Good Witch-
> *Wizard of Oz*

CHAPTER 14

My Final Thought
(at least for this book...)

All I Want for Christmas is...

A I am walking our three Shih Tzus down the street. Yep, how did you guess? I am trying to get them to poop. Why not open AND close the book with a dog pooping story? I bet that has never been done before.

Anyhow,

As I was walking them and managing the dog poop situation, which is a special skill, I had an epiphany......

I don't need any material gifts or gift cards for Christmas.

Instead, my wish list is this:
My husband, Ryan:

- Stay on the positive railroad tracks.
- Don't let past failures creep up on him. Stop it at the door.
- Shake off other people's poor behavior.

Me:

- Continue to make sure my energy is always clean.
- Not worry about what others think and forge my own path.
- Continue to watch my tone and reactions.

As a couple:

- Continue to look at everything as an opportunity that is meant for us and is good. One door, even if it gets shut, leads to another door.
- Continue to trust and build our intuition.
- Continue to dream big, manifest, and recognize The Law of Attraction.
- Continue to be grateful to everything and for everyone.

And here is why I made those Christmas wish lists....

Because shifting your mindset and belief system to the above builds the confidence for the limitless abundance you were meant to have. If you follow that truth, you can be as abundant and generous as you desire! So, start with something free but not easy for everyone. And make it communication.

Take the time to have open, honest, nonjudgmental conversations with your partner on a regular basis. The more you can do this, the easier it will be to open up to each other more frequently.

I learned a lot writing this book and then asking Ryan to read it. I thought "I knew it all"....I did not. There were extra stories and thought processes that came out of him reading the first draft, which I layered in. I was amazed at his confidence in allowing me to layer them in. Things I didn't realize, i.e., his reason for quitting drinking and his frustration which led to the "laundry bin incident." BTW- he has gotten much better at tossing his clothes in the bin. *I have to pinch myself...*

When I first picked the subtitle, Roadmap to a More Intimate Relationship, I was hopeful that people wouldn't assume it was a sex book.

Maybe someday, but, "not today." (Arya- Game of Thrones)

Real intimacy is when you and your partner can share anything without judgment or arguments but with love, compassion, an open mind, and an open heart. Actually listen and understand. The majority of people can go on vacation and have a fun time, but when they come back to reality, do they know what their partner's hopes and dreams are for the future? Do they know theirs? Do you support each other? Have confidence in each other? Or do you stifle each other? Do you openly talk about things which are good as well as painful? Experiences from the past that have left you scarred and limited your belief system and subconscious mind? How do you support each other with those challenges and revelations? These are pertinent questions to think about regarding your relationship.

Intimacy is a deeper level of communication and it's a journey. Step by step, layer by layer.

That's where the work comes in, but it is possible. We know you can do it!

Simple, But Not Always Easy Tips, Tools and Methodologies

"Inaction is Expensive"—Unknown

I am sharing ideas which I have found to be beneficial over the years. Give yourself grace and compassion as you start to use them. Even if you cannot get your partner to participate, begin to implement these tips and tools yourself. Once you begin to see change, and then your partner starts to see a difference, momentum will pick up.

Keep in mind- Change doesn't happen overnight. You must remember to use these tools and keep going. This is where the majority of people fail. They do not do the work.

The daily practice is what's important!

1. **Start here**
   "I am....."

   Understanding yourself all starts with you and your thoughts:

   a. What are you saying to yourself?
   b. What is your partner saying to themselves?

2. **Affirmation Rampage**

Abraham Hicks, as well as many other coaches and teachers, often recommend doing an affirmation rampage. A rampage is where you have a list- this can be either written down or in your brain- of positive affirmations, and you say them for a few minutes to get your energy to shift. In other words, instead of saying "I am successful" one time, turn it into an affirmation that you say over and over. The goal is to feel good with "I Am" statements and believe them, hence changing your subconscious brain patterns.

You can say something such as:

- I am healthy
- I am loved
- I am successful
- I am abundant
- My business is growing
- My book is a #1 bestseller
- I am generous
- I am prosperous

When I first started, I looked to other authors and coaches for ideas, then memorized ones I related to and tweaked them for myself. There are plenty of ideas on Pinterest, YouTube, and other social platforms. Journal and create a list over time.

3. **Breathing**

This is a fantastic breathing technique from ISAMIZU Global, courtesy of Dr. Isabel Perez and Dr. Jyun Shimizu, called "Your Quantum Nature (YQN) Technique™".

This breathing technique is simple to remember and will help you relax and calm your nervous system. With proper breathing, belly breathing, you activate the vagus nerve, which is the nerve in the body that stimulates the Parasympathetic Nervous System or the body's relaxation response. You do not want to breathe from the chest.

If you are a woman, start the exercise with your left hand. If you are a man, begin with the right hand.

Take your index finger from your opposite hand, bring it to the top of your middle finger, and gently drag it down to your forearm. Repeat.

Repeat as many times as you would like or need to; we recommended at least five times on each side.

As you do the movement, breathe in- while saying or thinking positive thoughts or words you wish to allow.

Still doing the movement, as you breath out, say or think negative words you wish to release.

Example: breathe in- peace, breathe out- comparison.

You are replacing the negative emotions with positive emotions and starting to rewire your brain to allow positive attitude pathways to develop.

4. **Meditation**

I started meditating in June, 2018, and have never missed a day. Now, if I can, I meditate 2-3 times a day for 20 minutes each. The benefits of meditation are above and beyond what I can express.

There are countless meditation tools available online, apps, YouTube videos, etc. I prefer high-frequency music and the guided meditations I mention below. An excellent app to get started with is Insight Timer. The main objective is to find what you connect with and do it every day.

My recommended podcasts about meditation on the Good Karma Success Coach Podcast are guided meditations from spiritual teacher Debbra Lupien; episodes #60, 72, 82, and 105. Episodes where I share my thoughts and tips on meditation are #2 and 49.

5. **Values- To Do/ To Be**

Each of you separately makes two lists and then review them together.

- One list is- To Do
- One list is- To Be

Separate the two values:

- To Do contains the actual things we usually think of- call the insurance agent, file our taxes, pick up the kids from soccer, plan a vacation.
- To Be is along the lines of peaceful, well-rested, healthy, loved, compassionate.

Bonus:

- Take it one step further and create a To Do List for The Universe and let it go. I first heard this at an Abraham Hicks event and thought it was genius!

6. **Questions to ask yourself and your partner to think about and journal**

These questions should be reviewed and revisited. The answers may not come to you right away, and that's okay. Some of this may be new thinking and could bring up patterns and past situations. I am the queen of burying bad situations, so you are not alone. If they are situations, challenges, or patterns that you are continually thinking about, hopefully this will help you release them.

It's even more beneficial if you can talk about them first together and then release them. Releasing old situations will help you feel lighter, more at ease, less anxiety, peaceful, and accomplished. When you start to realize the benefits of releasing, you may want to make it a habit. The lighter your energy can be, the happier you become.

Again, this takes time and practice, so give yourself grace and allow the process to guide you.

1. What situation in the last day did I feel bad about? (Something you did)
2. What is a situation in the last day that triggered my emotions?
   a. Week?
   b. Month?
   c. Year?
      i. How did that make me feel?
      ii. How did I handle it?

        iii. How did I feel after I handled it?

        iv. What was my next step?

3. What are your weaknesses? It is important to be very honest here.

4. What are your strengths?

5. How can you make your weaknesses into a game/laugh/have fun?

Plan some time together to celebrate both weaknesses and strengths.

7. Bucket Tool

Years ago, when I was a Senior Buyer in the corporate world, I found my mind naturally categorizing, aka *bucketing*, challenges I was having. The challenges could be regarding team members, business ideas, strategies, or prioritizing how I would get through my day.

When I stopped and recognized what was going on vs. operating on autopilot, and then took a few minutes to think about it and how I felt, I could release the extra energy and move forward.

Deciding what to do and how to handle the situation took the pressure off. Most people react to situations and then often regret their reactions. I was definitely "that" person and decided to make some changes.

As I have moved from being a corporate buyer into sales, I found I was using my *Bucket Tool* and thought process more and more.

It has also become natural, and I find myself talking about it. The word buckets have become part of my natural speak. So, what does this look like and how can you start to apply this tool?

Visualize three buckets-

Bucket 1 is virtually a **no change** bucket.
Bucket 2 is **moderate** change.
Bucket 3 is **severe** change.

You can use this tool for business or personal purposes. Virtually any situation which appears challenging, stressful, or needs some extra consideration can use this valuable tool. Once you practice, like anything, it becomes second nature, and your mindset will quickly shift to this productive way to resolve an issue. You will start to build more confidence in your ability to handle anything with ease. The key is to keep in mind how you are feeling by stopping and recognizing the situation.

Contact Melinda Van Fleet and/or Ryan Van Fleet For:

- Private One on One Coaching
- Professional Speaking Opportunities

Email at info@melindavanfleet.com

Connect Further with Melinda Van Fleet:

Facebook: https://www.facebook.com/melinda.vanfleet.315
Linked In: https://www.linkedin.com/in/melinda-van-fleet/
Instagram: https://www.instagram.com/melinda_vanfleet/
Website: https://goodkarmasuccesscoach.com

Coming Early Summer 2021

Life and Love Lessons
How to Discover Confidence Through Your Spiritual Journey

If you enjoyed this book, please tell a friend and leave a rating and review on Amazon. Thank you!

Acknowledgments

Many years ago, when Ryan and I first got together, I started saying a prayer every night thanking our family, friends, connections- and now our three dogs. That prayer continues with my heartfelt thanks!

Thank you to every person in my life that has influenced me, good and bad. You learn a lot from the bad, and sometimes more than the good. I appreciate your support and am aware it doesn't always happen. Hence the people who are supportive are even more special. You know who you are. Good Karma.

I also dedicate this to my team that lovingly guides me every day. When times have been tough, I always know I can rely on my spirit team to guide me toward the rainbows. I am blessed and grateful. Never enough words.

With love and gratitude- thank you all for reading this book!

Melinda

Melinda & Ryan Van Fleet:
Success Coaches | Professional Speakers |
Small Business Owners and an
Obsessed Sportfishing Captain

Melinda and Ryan Van Fleet lost their corporate jobs at the same time in 2009. Instead of focusing on their setback, they packed their belongings and headed to The Florida Keys to begin the second act they had envisioned.

Ryan Van Fleet built his successful fishing charter business *Good Karma Sportfishing*, podcast *Good Karma Sportfishing Podcast,* and thriving community, based on the values of persistence, confidence, collaboration, having fun, and catching big fish!

Melinda Van Fleet is a multi-passionate success coach who built her coaching, speaking, and writing on the values of helping others believe in themselves and take action. Melinda believes many women are stuck and unfulfilled their potential. Host of the podcasts *Good Karma Success Coach* and *Confident Conversations.*

Together they make a powerful team helping empower individuals and couples to live their best lives. They strongly believe that if they can do it, you can do it too.

Contact at info@melindavanfleet.com

Made in the USA
Columbia, SC
06 March 2021